T0120483

Nick Harrison

All Scripture quotations are from the King James Version.

Cover design by Dugan Design Group
Cover image © Tony Craddock / Adobe Stock
Interior design by Aesthetic Soup, Jeff Jansen

For bulk, special sales, or ministry purchases, please call 1-800-547-8979.
Email: CustomerService@hhpbooks.com

KJV Devotional from the Psalms

Published by Harvest House Publishers
Eugene, Oregon 97408
www.harvesthousepublishers.com

ISBN 978-0-7369-8935-0 (hardcover)
ISBN 978-0-7369-8936-7 (eBook)

Library of Congress Control Number: 2023951653

Printed in China

24 25 26 27 28 29 30 31 32 / RDS / 10 9 8 7 6 5 4 3 2 1

INTRODUCTION

The book of Psalms is my favorite book in the Bible. There I can find comfort, encouragement, sympathy in times of doubt, and many exhortations to praise God (can praise be mentioned too often? I think not!).

David, of course, wrote many of the psalms, and in doing so he reveals his victories in God but also his doubts, questions, and frustrations. In other words, David was much like us. The other psalmists were also revealing as they put their worship of the Lord into poetry and song.

This centuries-old book has been cherished by readers from ages past. Often sung, the book has stood the test of time, not only among fellow Christians but also among secular readers, who have remarked on its excellence. It has stood the test of time because its words reflect the human condition so well.

On the following pages you'll find at least one devotion from each of the 150 psalms. In some cases, you'll find several devotions based on one psalm—as with Psalm 119, for example, which with its 176 verses offers us multiple days of devotions.

As you read the portion of the psalm, make it your own. Pray it. Internalize it. Make it relevant to you. We know, for instance, that David wrote Psalm 51 as a prayer of repentance after he murdered Uriah in order to take Bathsheba to satisfy his lust. Though your experience is different, surely you will, like all of us, find cause to petition the Lord:

Have mercy upon me, O God, according to thy lovingkindness: according unto the multitude of thy tender mercies blot out my transgressions. Wash me throughly from mine iniquity, and cleanse me from my sin. For I acknowledge my transgressions: and my sin is ever before me. Against thee, thee only, have I sinned, and done this evil in thy sight: that thou mightest be justified when thou speakest, and be clear when thou judgest.

Psalm 51:1-4

As you read the chosen verse and devotional, my fellow psalm lovers, it's my prayer that if you read in the morning, it will encourage you through the day, or it will bring you restful sleep if read at the end of your day.

Come with me now, into our beloved book of Psalms in the classic King James Version.

BLESSED

Blessed is the man that walketh not in the counsel of the ungodly, nor standeth in the way of sinners, nor sitteth in the seat of the scornful.
But his delight is in the law of the LORD; and in his law doth he meditate day and night.
And he shall be like a tree planted by the rivers of water, that bringeth forth his fruit in his season; his leaf also shall not wither; and whatsoever he doeth shall prosper.

PSALM 1:1-3

Among the many promises in the Bible, some of the best are found in Psalm 1. The promises, though, are to those who avoid the counsel of the ungodly, who do not consort with unbelievers or join their voice to the scornful. Instead, our delight is to be in the law of the Lord day and night. The result? We shall be like a fruitful tree planted by the rivers of water. And whatever we do shall prosper. What a glorious promise!

Lord, my desire is to prosper according to your will for my life. My delight is in you and your law. I do not listen to the naysayers—the mockers and scorners. Neither do I accept the counsel of the ungodly. Your Holy Spirit is my guide, advocate, helper, and counselor. May I have ears to hear and a heart to obey.

Today's Takeaway

A blessed life is a life that delights in the law of the Lord.

THE FATE OF UNBELIEVERS

The ungodly are not so: but are like the chaff
which the wind driveth away.
Therefore the ungodly shall not stand in the judgment,
nor sinners in the congregation of the righteous.
For the LORD knoweth the way of the righteous:
but the way of the ungodly shall perish.
PSALM 1:4-6

God sees only two kinds of people, the godly and the ungodly. The former have taken upon themselves the righteousness of Christ, and they are thus free from the penalty and power of their sins. The latter are those who depend on their own righteousness—or feel no need for righteousness at all. The godly have an eternal destiny, gifted to them by God. The ungodly shall perish in their sins, forever lost.

Father, this life is not all there is. You have ordained eternal life for every person. But where that eternity will be spent depends on whether we are clothed with the righteousness of Christ or stand naked due to the rags of our own righteousness. Lord, you know the way of the righteous, but woe to those who shall perish in their sins.

Give me, O God, a heart for the lost!

Today's Takeaway

God knows the way of the righteous. In Christ, I am righteous.

Serve and Rejoice

Serve the Lord with fear, and rejoice with trembling.
Psalm 2:11

We who believe are called to be the Lord's servants—and we do so with godly fear, trembling on the one hand and yet rejoicing on the other for the opportunity to be included among God's servers.

In serving him, we find no reluctance or exhaustion. In truth, we are strengthened and empowered by fulfilling our earthly assignments, looking forward to the day when we shall at last be in the presence of the One we have served. Until then, we have the vital presence of the Holy Spirit within us.

Lord, who am I that you should choose me to be numbered among your servants? I tremble with godly fear at your goodness, even as I rejoice with great happiness that you take note of me and desire to use me in your kingdom, both in this present life and in the life to come.

Father, never let me take for granted the great privilege of being your child—and your servant. When you lead me in a new direction, guide my uncertain steps along the way.

I do long for the day I shall be forever in your presence.

Today's Takeaway

It is a divine privilege to be God's servant.

THE LORD, MY SHIELD

LORD, how are they increased that trouble me!
many are they that rise up against me.
Many there be which say of my soul, There
is no help for him in God. Selah.
But thou, O LORD, art a shield for me; my
glory, and the lifter up of mine head.
PSALM 3:1-3

God inserts himself as a shield between us and our adversaries. Though others may aim their arrows at us, God intercepts them. He defies all of those who say there is no help for us with the Lord—that God has forgotten us or doesn't care that we are in trouble.

When tempted to doubt or be brought low by our circumstances or adversaries, he is there to lift our head, to comfort and console us. If dark days lie ahead, we need have no fear. God shall be a shield for us. He is forever our glory and the lifter of our head.

Dear Lord, there are days when trouble seems to surround me, when adversaries assail me, and I don't know where to turn. But even on such days and in the presence of those who mock my trust in you, you are there to shield me from their arrows. You watch over me in trouble, and you even order circumstances to my favor. You lift my head in triumph in the face of apparent defeat.

You, Father, are my true glory. To you belongs all the praise!

Today's Takeaway

God is a shield between me and my troubles.

I Am Set Apart

Know that the LORD hath set apart him that is godly for himself: the LORD will hear when I call unto him.

Psalm 4:3

Through one divine action in saving us, God has set us apart both individually and collectively as his church—literally "called-out ones." His setting us apart was *for himself.*

When we are tempted to doubt our worth, we need only to consider the cross where God spoke loudly in affirming that we are worth the life of his dear Son.

In setting us apart, he has covenanted to hear our prayers. We need only to call out to him. He will hear. He will answer.

O Lord, you have set me apart for yourself. What manner of love is this? There is nothing in me that warrants such lavish affection—and yet your very nature of love has sought me out and has found me, taken me in as your beloved child. You have given ear to my many prayers as only a loving father would do. For this, I worship you.

Dear Father, never let me wander from your love. Never let me forget whose I am.

Today's Takeaway

God has set me apart for himself.

I Dwell in Safety

I will both lay me down in peace, and sleep: for thou,
Lord, only makest me dwell in safety...
I will not be afraid of ten thousands of people, that
have set themselves against me round about.
Psalm 4:8; 3:6

Our God is a 24-7 God. He is always there, always *here*. He watches over us, even as we sleep, oblivious to his nightly care. We dwell in safety when we dwell in his presence. We lie down in peace. Our troubles may be many, our foes giants, our hopes as dim as dusk—and yet in the face of the largest problems, our Creator is with us. If we can trust God for one troubling circumstance, we can trust him for ten thousand troubles. The size of a challenge is of no consequence to the Lord—large or small, he is with us.

Father, you are my God in all circumstances, both large and small. So great is your care for me that I'm able to lie down in peace, knowing that as I sleep, you keep watch. Even when my mind temporarily forgets my troubling situation, you are at work formulating the desired end of my problem. Thank you, Lord, for your constant care.

Today's Takeaway

I can trust God in any situation.

Shout for Joy!

Let all those that put their trust in thee rejoice: let them ever shout for joy, because thou defendest them: let them also that love thy name be joyful in thee.

Psalm 5:11

Though many Christians are consumed with fear and worry, they need not stay there. In this verse we see an admonition to rejoice and a call to shout for joy, concluding with a command that all who love his name should be joyful in him. We may have the same challenges the unsaved world has, but our advantage—our cause to rejoice in our circumstances—is that our joy is found in him. And no adversity on earth can change that.

O Lord, I do put my trust in you and you alone. I rejoice in your watchful eye over me. I shout for joy because you defend me against all charges of the enemy and all the schemes of those who want to see me fail. Above all, I love your name, O Lord. I rejoice in you and all that you are. I have faith, Father, that you will see me through every earthly trial. You are my righteous defender.

Today's Takeaway

It is God's command that I rejoice in him.

The Favor of the Lord

Thou, LORD, wilt bless the righteous; with favor wilt thou compass him as with a shield.

Psalm 5:12

We who believe not only have God as our protective shield, but we also enjoy the favor of the Lord. Behind the scenes of daily life, God orchestrates events to our good. His favor acts as a shield surrounding us, guarding us. Because of his benevolence, we are blessed. We have no reason to despair or doubt. After all, we are safely on his path, not that rugged trail of our own misguided choices. And our Creator also gives us favor with others. It's not unusual for him to intervene in a transaction and give us favor with the other party. In evangelism, we may be surprised as God gives us favor with unbelievers.

Thank you, Lord for your blessing on the righteous—those who are righteous by faith, not by works. Thank you for the divine favor that compasses me as a shield. Because of your blessing and your favor, I'm able to step out in faith, reaching for the destiny you have for me while I live for you. Guide my steps, Father. Let your blessing and favor remain on me all my days.

Today's Takeaway

I enjoy the favor of God!

He Hears My Groans; He Sees My Tears

Have mercy upon me, O Lord; for I am weak:
O Lord, heal me; for my bones are vexed…
I am weary with my groaning; all the night make I my bed to swim;
I water my couch with my tears.

Psalm 6:2, 6

Every Christian has experienced seasons filled with tears. We groan, we cry, we even doubt. In our bed, we fail to sleep for want of peace. And where is God in such times? He is right there with us, hearing our groans, accepting our tears. And just when things are at their lowest, our Creator turns a corner for us and brings peace as we cease our tears and rest in the surety that he is in control—even in this hard situation.

Through it all, God's mercy is upon us. As our deliverer, he heals us in our weakness, and his holy Word makes our vexed bones whole. All our hopes are fully met in him.

God, I am in need of your great mercy. In my weakness, I cry out for your healing touch. My bones ache for lack of strength. My groans spring from my lips to your ears. Though my bed is wet with tears, you bring new life through your comforting Holy Spirit. My trust in you sets all things aright.

Today's Takeaway

At my lowest, I find God is there for me. His mercies are mine.

I Will Sing Praise

I will praise the Lord *according to his righteousness: and will sing praise to the name of the* Lord *most high.*

Psalm 7:17

Christians are born-again praisers. In sadness, in happiness, we praise him according to his righteousness. No matter how many years of life God grants us, we will never tire of praising him, nor will we run out of words. Our hearts are full of worship, and when we open our mouths, our tongues readily proclaim his praise.

When we are low, we groan and cry out to the Lord for relief. When we see God bring victory into our lives, we are quick to praise him. But the secret to a happy life is to develop the habit of praising God in all things—not *for* all things, but *in* all things. There is no circumstance we will face that does not carry with it God's solution. When trials come, our response is to praise in spite of the trial, and through the trial, as we trust our Creator for the coming solution—his solution—which is often revealed *as* we praise.

Lord, remind me to glorify you in all things. I'm quick to praise when there are no trials, or at the happy end of a trial, but I also see the need to praise you during the trial. I know that your Holy Spirit within me is a spirit of praise, so help me to obey the Spirit's urge to be a person of praise—in all things.

—m—

Today's Takeaway

It's in my spiritual DNA to be one of God's praisers.

Crowned with Glory and Honor

When I consider thy heavens, the work of thy fingers, the moon and the stars, which thou hast ordained; what is man, that thou art mindful of him? and the son of man, that thou visitest him? For thou hast made him a little lower than the angels, and hast crowned him with glory and honor. Thou madest him to have dominion over the works of thy hands; thou hast put all things under his feet.

Psalm 8:3-6

Is it not amazing that God has created all of mankind and each of us with individual care? And after creating us, he remains mindful of us through our entire lives. He visits us with his presence, even when we're unaware. Still more, he crowns us with glory and honor. How can we not love and praise our wonderful Lord?

Father, once again I ponder your greatness and my smallness. And yet even in my insignificance, you find value equal to the life of your Son. He was the perfect lamb sacrificed for my sins, an event of great significance. And indeed, you count all that happens to me as significant. You have turned insignificance into great significance. For this, and for all you are, I praise you.

Today's Takeaway

Though I am small, God is mindful of me.

With My Whole Heart Will I Praise Thee

I will praise thee, O Lord, with my whole heart;
I will show forth all thy marvelous works.
I will be glad and rejoice in thee: I will sing
praise to thy name, O thou most High.

Psalm 9:1-2

God is not looking for halfhearted praisers. Nor should we accept the role of part-time praisers. Rather, we approach the Lord with high praise, unending praise, full-hearted praise. Our full praises make us glad, and we rejoice in him.

As you worship God today, let your heart overflow with words of goodness to the God of marvelous works.

Lord, sometimes I just don't have the words to rightly praise you. In fact, there are no words that satisfy my longing to adore and worship you. You fill my heart with praise, and I bring forth the best I know to utter—and yet it doesn't seem to be enough. You have given me so much, and you have entrusted me with showing forth your marvelous works. Father, as I offer my hands for those works, guide me. As I speak the praise in my heart, give me the words I find so elusive.

To you be the glory!

Today's Takeaway

My heart overflows with praise to God!

Our Righteous Judge

The Lord shall endure for ever: he hath prepared his throne for judgment. And he shall judge the world in righteousness, he shall minister judgment to the people in uprightness.

Psalm 9:7-8

We need never fear the judgment of God if our hope is in Christ alone. God's coming judgment is righteous and fair. No one can ever lay a charge of injustice to the Lord, nor can any say to him, "That's unfair!" God has given the way of escape to all who have ears to hear. The Lord reigns forever. His throne is prepared for righteous judgment.

Father, if truth be told, your righteous judgment of me would find me cast off from your presence forever. But with you, there is mercy, there is grace, there is life eternal. Your judgment of me is based on my standing in Christ. For this, I'm forever grateful. I have no fear of being cast off, but I instead look forward to being in your presence forever: all judgment passed, all judgment placed on Christ.

Lord, I thank you in your upright judgment. You shall surely endure forever.

Today's Takeaway

All of God's judgments are righteous because he is righteous.

Where Are You, Lord?

Why standest thou afar off, O Lord? why hidest thou thyself in times of trouble?

Psalm 10:1

Every Christian has known times of trouble. Some seasons were short and passed quickly. Others lingered on, perhaps for years. Our cries to God seemed to reach no higher than the clouds. It was as if we were crossing an endless desert. We questioned the Lord, we begged for relief, we wondered at his silence.

But in all our trials, we are not alone. Even mighty men and women in the Bible passed through that same desert. We can hear David cry out, "Why standest thou afar off? Why hidest thou in my time of trouble?" But we are blessed to know that God *did* rescue David. His desert, like ours, ended at God's appointed time. Know that God is *not* far off. He is with you. He hides not.

Father, my seasons of trial have been hard. Yes, I've made it through. Yes, I'm still here, and I know that future trials and tribulations are in my path. But I also know that path leads directly to you and that, as I walk through the fiery trial, you will be with me, urging me to trust once again. No, you do not hide from me in trouble. You hear my cries, even those filled with doubt. Father, trusting you always enables me to take that next step on the stony path.

Today's Takeaway

God is ever present in my trials, even when I don't feel his presence.

The God Who Hears

Arise, O Lord; O God, lift up thine hand: forget not the humble...
Lord, thou hast heard the desire of the humble:
thou wilt prepare their heart, thou wilt cause thine ear to hear.
Psalm 10:12, 17

We know that God hears our words in times of need, but do we remember that he hears our desires—even those that are unspoken?

In his wisdom, he often withholds the granting of our desires until he has properly prepared our hearts. Yes, he does indeed hear our desires, both spoken and unspoken. And the condition for his lifted hand? That we be humble—not just in our words but in our actions. If we are proud, God has ways to humble us if we won't humble ourselves.

Humble ones, trust him. He hears your cry. Time will reveal his faithfulness.

Dear Lord, prepare my heart to receive the blessings you have for me. Show me where I need to change in order to better serve you. Remind me of your past faithfulness to me. When I'm proud, bring about the circumstances that will humble me. For if I'm proud, I block your blessings. Humility removes the barrier to blessing.

May Jesus be my role model.

Today's Takeaway

God hears the desires of the humble.

The Vital Foundations

If the foundations be destroyed, what can the righteous do?...For the righteous LORD loveth righteousness; his countenance doth behold the upright.

Psalm 11:3, 7

Foundations are essential in many aspects of life. That's especially true regarding our spiritual life. Is Christ the foundation of our faith? Is the Word of God foundational? Is prayer foundational to all aspects of our life?

If our idea of faith is based on emotions—on how we feel—we have a weak foundation. If we allow the bedrock of our faith to be undermined or destroyed, there is little we can do—except reestablish a right foundation based on the truth of the Bible and not the supposed wisdom of our critics or our fleeting feelings.

We must never forget God's love for the righteous man or woman. His countenance is upon them.

God, I see the need for firm foundations in all I do. I see that prayer is foundational to my well-being, my health, my finances, my relationships, and all that I am. Removing prayer from my life would be akin to tearing down the foundation to a mighty fortress—nothing of value can be built without a strong basis.

Today, I renew my commitment to a life founded on prayer.

Today's Takeaway

The Word of God is my foundation.

God Hates Violence

The Lord trieth the righteous: but the wicked and him that loveth violence his soul hateth.

Psalm 11:5

God hates violence, and his face is turned away from those who love it. He labels such people as wicked. There is hope for the violent only if they turn from their wicked ways and trust in the Lord. To do so, they must lay down their weapons of violence and pursue peace. Therein they will find the happiness that eluded them in their pursuit of brutality.

Father, you try me as a righteous Christian (righteous through Christ). Thus, I find my gift of righteousness holds firm and brings me great peace. As for violence, I renounce all my brutal ways, past and present.

Give me a heart to speak peace to those who are driven by anger and aggression. I pray they can lay down their weapons and seek the peace of the Holy Spirit. I pray they can exchange their hatred for love by coming to know your love. I pray, too, that they may come to know true joy, a product of a mind at peace and rest with you, O Lord.

Today's Takeaway

I stand for peace, not for violence.

The End of Flattering Lips

Help, Lord; for the godly man ceaseth; for the faithful
fail from among the children of men.
They speak vanity every one with his neighbor: with
flattering lips and with a double heart do they speak.
The Lord shall cut off all flattering lips, and
the tongue that speaketh proud things:
Who have said, With our tongue will we prevail;
our lips are our own: who is lord over us?

Psalm 12:1-4

Each of us must answer the question "Who is lord over me?" The prideful speak in defense of themselves; they believe their flattering lips will prevail in the day of God's judgment. But the Lord has the final say, and his response is to cut off the flattering lips and the proud tongue. We should, then, be watchful over our own tongues. We must be counted as faithful among the children of men.

Lord, the tongue is a deceitful part of the human body—mine included. I pray you will keep a watch over my lips. May I speak not vanity, but truth. Not pride, but humility. May you be Lord over all of my life, including my lips.

Today's Takeaway

God is Lord over every aspect of my life.

The Pure Words of the Lord

The words of the LORD are pure words: as silver tried in a furnace of earth, purified seven times.
PSALM 12:6

It doesn't take long for us to discover that the words of our fellow humans are occasionally faulty, even downright untrue. Sometimes we might even find that true of our own words. But God is not like man. The Lord's words are always true, edifying, and trustworthy. His words are pure. His words are right, never wrong. His words give us courage and strength to live the plan He has designed for us.

Always trust the pure words of the Creator. Take them into your heart. Meditate often on the words of the Lord.

God, I've lived long enough to know that the words of man are prone to error, pride, and impurity. May that not be true of me. Cleanse my heart of all impurity. Put my lips through the furnace that purifies.

By your Holy Spirit, lead me to speak uplifting words. May I be an encourager of others through the words I speak.

Teach me, Lord, through your *Word. Hide the pure Word in my heart.*

Today's Takeaway

God's words are pure; they are as silver to me.

How Long, O Lord?

How long wilt thou forget me, O Lord? for ever?
how long wilt thou hide thy face from me?
How long shall I take counsel in my soul, having sorrow in my heart daily? how long shall mine enemy be exalted over me?

Psalm 13:1-2

So many of the psalms are hymns of praise. It seems striking, then, to find among them one of David's laments. But the truth is that though we live lives of praise to God, sometimes we need to lament, knowing the Lord hears our cries as well as our praises. God did not forget David. Far from it. The Lord was with David throughout his life—even on the hard days when David despaired of life itself.

Today, you may take your petitions to God wondering if he's listening. Yes, he hears. He heard the first time you prayed over this situation, and he hears today's lament as well.

Keep praying. Keep crying out to the Lord. His ear is open to you.

Lord, it's hard to read of David's fear that you may have forgotten him. We know the rest of David's story, and no, you did not forget him. Nor do you forget me, even on those difficult days when it seems as if you've hidden your face from me. My joy is knowing that, as with David, you know the rest of the story of my life and have arranged for the successful outcome that has my name on it. You will never let my enemies be exalted over me.

Today's Takeaway

God hears my laments as well as my praises.

Bountiful Blessings Are Mine

I will sing unto the Lord, because he hath dealt bountifully with me.

Psalm 13:6

How does God deal with man? The psalmist declares that God has dealt bountifully with him. The Lord has not been stingy—nor can he be. God's nature is always to *give*—and that bountifully. And with what result? That we sing our praises to the Lord for his amazing generosity. We, too, are to follow our Lord's example and give to others bountifully.

Lord, you are a generous God. Your nature is to give, and likewise your instruction to us is to give, assuring us that it's more blessed to give than to receive. Surely, then, it blesses you to give—and give bountifully.

I have needs, dear Lord, but you know them all. You care for me as a loving father. You arrange for every need—and even some wants—to be met bountifully. So, Lord, like the psalmist I will sing unto you for past bountiful blessings as well as the blessings I have now and the blessings to come from you in the days ahead.

Wonderful, giving Father, I praise you!

Today's Takeaway

My life is bountiful because my Lord is a generous giver.

The Folly of Atheism

The fool hath said in his heart, There is no God.
Psalm 14:1

To deny the Creator, we must close our eyes to much evidence to the contrary. Nature calls out the existence of God. The stars, the seasons, and the very existence of life on earth declare his being. No human has the truth of God's existence hidden from them. In fact, the Lord openly displays his handiwork as evidence of himself. Further, his giving of Christ for our sins displays his deep love for us. Atheism is a foolish attempt to set aside the voice of God, who will not abide divine competition, in favor of the voice of self.

God, the atheist apparently needs more proof of your existence than you've already given through creation. I need no such further evidence. I see your existence not just in nature but in the visible and invisible blessings you've brought to me. I see your hand in the many prayers you've answered. I know miracles exist. I know there is a heaven when I leave this life. Truly, Lord, the world has its fill of fools who deny you. May their number decrease as they awaken from their self-imposed slumber and behold the ample evidence of your existence that surrounds them daily.

Today's Takeaway

To disbelieve in God, one must close his or her eyes to reality.

I Shall Never Be Moved

Lord, who shall abide in thy tabernacle? who shall dwell in thy holy hill?
He that walketh uprightly, and worketh righteousness,
and speaketh the truth in his heart.
He that backbiteth not with his tongue, nor doeth evil to his neighbor, nor taketh up a reproach against his neighbor. In whose eyes a vile person is contemned; but he honoreth them that fear the LORD. *He that sweareth to his own hurt, and changeth not. He that putteth not out his money to usury, nor taketh reward against the innocent. He that doeth these things shall never be moved.*

Psalm 15:1-5

The list of requirements to abide with God isn't long—and it's quite doable. And yet so many fail to meet the requirements. Our righteousness, after all, is as filthy rags. We don't always live as we should. Is it any wonder, then, that we are occasionally "moved"? And yet the promise is that if we live righteous lives, we shall never be moved. How, then, is this possible? Only through a divinely appointed substitute—the Lord Jesus Christ. All who trust in him shall indeed *never* be moved.

O Lord, I do trust in you. I desire above all else to abide with you in your heavenly tabernacle. Your holy hill is my destination. I therefore live out the righteousness of Christ. I will walk uprightly, speak the truth. I honor those who fear you, God. I do all things according to your will, Father.

Today's Takeaway

Daily I walk out my righteous standing
with God by living righteously.

God Has Chosen the Best for Me

The lines are fallen unto me in pleasant places;
yea, I have a goodly heritage.
Psalm 16:6

Whether we're young or old, when we look back on our years, can we not see that the lines have fallen to us in pleasant places? Yes, there has been grief—no doubt with more to come. But life cannot be defined by our sorrows and heartaches. Rather, God would have us take note of our joys—of the lines that have fallen to us in pleasant places.

Yes, we do indeed have a goodly heritage.

Father, indeed the lines of life have fallen unto me in pleasant places. In you I have a goodly heritage. I can look back at the road behind me and see how you helped me navigate the bumps and unexpected turns. The hills have been hard to traverse, but on the other side, I was able to coast for a while. Lord, my life is a great gift for which I am most thankful. I will have more surprises along the way, some easy and pleasant, others hard and troubling. And yet through it all I declare that the lines have fallen to me in pleasant places.

Today's Takeaway

God has seen to it that the lines have fallen to me in my favor.

The Lord Is at My Right Hand

I have set the Lord always before me: because he is at my right hand, I shall not be moved. Therefore my heart is glad, and my glory rejoiceth: my flesh also shall rest in hope.

Psalm 16:8-9

Why are we occasionally "moved"? Is it not because we have momentarily forgotten the nearness of the Lord? Have we not set him before us? After all, the psalmist noted that setting the Lord before him was an "always" need.

Yes, God is at our right hand, and we need not be moved. But to catch the wind, a boat must set its sails. So too must we believers, by faith, set the Lord before us.

Lord, I desire stability. I desire a faith that is immovable. For that reason, I set you always before me. You abide at my right hand, keeping me upright. Keeping me stable through life's events—both good and bad.

When I wander from the path or momentarily forget your presence, please remind me. Wake me by whatever means necessary to restore my balance, since it's only when I'm stable in my faith that I'm useful in helping others. And when I'm balanced and secure, may I help others stabilize in their faith.

Thank you, Lord, for stability in Christ!

Today's Takeaway

Daily I set the Lord before me in all I do.

Fullness of Joy, Pleasures Forevermore

Thou wilt show me the path of life: in thy presence is fulness of joy; at thy right hand there are pleasures for evermore.

Psalm 16:11

Have we asked God to show us the path of life—or are we aimlessly walking on an indistinct route with no particular goal? When God gives us even a glimpse of our true path, what do we find? We discover fullness of joy and pleasures forevermore. For the path we're on is found in one place: at his right hand. Many Christians never really find this route, except to wander on it briefly before returning to the seemingly more comfortable path of least resistance.

Don't be content with a lesser plan B. Always go for God's plan A. That's where true joy resides.

Father, your promise is to show me the path of life. There I will find fullness of joy in your presence. In dwelling under the protection of your right hand, I will find pleasures forevermore. This, Lord, is a call to experience your joyful life. I gladly forsake the way of the world and its "joys" and instead accept your unfailing joys.

Today's Takeaway

I am living out God's plan A for my life, trusting him all the way.

The Paths of the Destroyer

Concerning the works of men, by the word of thy lips
I have kept me from the paths of the destroyer.
Psalm 17:4

Every Christian is on Satan's hit list. He is the would-be destroyer of whoever opts for his paths—the "paths of the destroyer." What, then, are we to do to avoid destruction? We must be wise enough to discern the paths of God from the paths of our satanic enemy. Regarding the latter, we must avoid his paths altogether. And if we discover we have somehow wandered onto his path, either willingly or blindly, we must at once depart and return to the way of the righteous—God's path of blessing.

Father, I know the destroyer of my faith and even my life has a strategy to bring me down. He lures me to his path with enticing temptations. Alas, he knows my weaknesses.

But he does not know the strength of my faith, and for that I thank you, Lord. I trust in your Word to keep me on your path of blessing, not his path of destruction. Speak through your Word, Father, and I will obey the word of your lips.

Today's Takeaway

I have a fierce enemy in the destroyer, but I keep away from his paths.

O God, Incline Thine Ear

Hold up my goings in thy paths, that my footsteps slip not.
I have called upon thee, for thou wilt hear me, O God:
incline thine ear unto me, and hear my speech.
Psalm 17:5-6

Eight billion people on earth and we wonder if God hears the prayers of the many that call on him. Yes, the Lord inclines his ear to every petition his children utter. He not only hears their prayers, but he also knows their every need before they pray. Such is our great God.

Pray today that the Lord would hold you up in your goings, that your foot would not slip. He will hear. His ear is inclined toward you.

Father, I depend on you to hold up my goings in thy paths, day by day. If you were to fail me, my footsteps would surely slip. But you are a God who hears. You know me inside and out. When I call on you, you incline your ear to me. You hear me as I offer my praises, enumerate my requests, surrender my fears and anxieties, and even boldly submit my questions. God, thank you for your ears to hear!

Today's Takeaway

God always inclines his ear to me.

THE LORD, MY STRENGTH

I will love thee, O LORD, my strength.
The LORD is my rock, and my fortress, and my deliverer;
my God, my strength, in whom I will trust; my buckler,
and the horn of my salvation, and my high tower.
PSALM 18:1-2

So often in the book of Psalms we are directed to take refuge in God. He is the only safe harbor during the storm. If he doesn't quiet the raging sea, he will stay with us until we reach a safe shore.

God is rock-solid for us. He is a formidable fortress, a divine deliverer—our very strength in whom we trust.

Run to him in every stormy occasion. He is our high tower.

God, there is such great joy in loving you. By loving you, I am loving my source of strength. I find in you a rock, a fortress, and a deliverer. For all the storms that come my way, I trust in your goodness. You are my buckler, the horn of my salvation—and yes, my high tower to which I run in times of trouble.

Yes, Lord, I love you, my strength.

Today's Takeaway

God is rock-solid for me.

THE LAW OF THE LORD

The law of the LORD is perfect, converting the soul:
the testimony of the LORD is sure, making wise the simple.
The statutes of the LORD are right, rejoicing the heart:
the commandment of the LORD is pure, enlightening the eyes.
The fear of the LORD is clean, enduring for ever:
the judgments of the LORD are true and righteous altogether.
More to be desired are they than gold, yea, than much fine gold:
sweeter also than honey and the honeycomb.
Moreover by them is thy servant warned: and in
keeping of them there is great reward.

PSALM 19:7-11

When God gives instructions for a blessed life, we must listen and obey. The Lord's law is perfect. His statutes are right, even to *rejoicing the heart.* His commandments are pure. The fear of the Lord is clean and endures forever. All that God is and has for us is to be ardently desired. There is great reward for the wise Christian who fears the Creator—and takes note of the warning of his Word.

Lord, not only are you perfect in every respect, but your law, too, is perfect. Your statutes are right—they rejoice the heart. Fearing you is cleansing; your righteous judgments are more desirable than gold and sweeter than honeycomb. Best of all, they serve as a warning to those who tend to wander and a promise of reward to those who obey your Word.

Today's Takeaway

God's statutes rejoice my heart.

PRESUMPTUOUS SINS

Keep back thy servant also from presumptuous sins; let them not have dominion over me: then shall I be upright, and I shall be innocent from the great transgression. Let the words of my mouth, and the meditation of my heart, be acceptable in thy sight, O LORD, my strength, and my redeemer.

PSALM 19:13-14

There is great transgression in our presumptuous sins. So subtle are they that if not dealt with early, they can have dominion over us and thus become all the more difficult to shed. A life void of presumptuous sins allows us to be upright and innocent before God.

We must watch our words. We must be careful what enters our hearts. Much of what we're offered daily is not acceptable and must be rejected, but that which is of good report is to be welcomed and meditated upon.

O Lord, save me from the subtle presumptuous sins that I may absentmindedly overlook. Deal with me quickly, lest those small sins grow into larger sins, having dominion over me. I long to be free from every failing, to be upright in your presence—innocent from all transgressions and righteous in your eyes because of my faith in my Redeemer.

Today's Takeaway

I'm careful to keep back from presumptuous sins.

His Saving Strength

We will rejoice in thy salvation, and in the name of our God we will set up our banners: the LORD fulfil all thy petitions. Now know I that the LORD saveth his anointed; he will hear him from his holy heaven with the saving strength of his right hand.

Psalm 20:5-6

We serve a Lord for whom we should raise banners proclaiming his glory. In fact, one of God's names as revealed in Exodus 17:15 is *Jehovah Nissi*, "the Lord, my banner." This God saves us, his anointed ones. He hears that prayer you utter today and upholds you with the power of his right hand.

Rejoice in your salvation! Raise the banners! Tell of his worthiness. He is our *Jehovah Nissi*.

Lord, you are worthy of praise, my Jehovah Nissi*! I rejoice in your salvation. I raise the banners of my heart. I tell again and again of your worthiness and bless your name. You are the God who hears from heaven. You save with the strength of your right hand. I rejoice in you, the God of my salvation, my redeemer, the giver of good gifts. I honor you, the everlasting One. Holy is your name!*

Today's Takeaway

Raise the banner of the Lord, for he is worthy!

IN GOD I TRUST

Some trust in chariots, and some in horses: but we
will remember the name of the LORD our God.
They are brought down and fallen: but we are risen, and stand upright.
PSALM 20:7-8

We have so many options today in which we can trust. In the psalmist's day, it was chariots and horses. Today we trust in banks, higher learning, artificial intelligence, the military, politics, the media—the list goes on.

The wise Christian, however, knows that our primary confidence is in the Lord. Someday the false recipients of our trust will crumble, and those who have trusted in them will wilt with discouragement. Not so for those who put their faith in the everlasting God. Our trust will never lead to disappointment.

Lord, today I stand upright while those who have relied on idols have fallen. I refuse to trust the false idols of this present age. They will all turn to dust in due time. But trusting in you, I will live forever. Other gods will fall, but you are the fountain of eternal life. Thank you, Father, for your trustworthiness.

Today's Takeaway

I trust only in the Lord, my God.

Rejoicing in Salvation

The king shall joy in thy strength, O Lord; and in thy salvation how greatly shall he rejoice! Thou hast given him his heart's desire, and hast not withholden the request of his lips.

Psalm 21:1-2

It's astonishing how God uses our desires to motivate us to pray for the very things our heavenly Father wants us to have. Our righteous desires become God's will as he brings to pass the good and necessary things to fulfill our destiny. In our salvation, we greatly rejoice!

Lord, what have you withheld from me? What desires are unfulfilled? None.

You know my needs, and you even consider my wants. And yet at no time have you left me without what I truly need. After all, what is my heart's desire but to experience more of you and live out your divine plan for my life. Whenever I deviate from that plan, you're there to steer me back onto the right path. And why? Because you delight in my God-assigned life as much as I do. Lord, let me not miss a minute of your guidance nor neglect an ounce of your provision. Father, I joy in your strength!

Today's Takeaway

I rejoice in my great salvation!

The God Who Delivers

Our fathers trusted in thee: they trusted, and thou didst deliver them. They cried unto thee, and were delivered: they trusted in thee, and were not confounded.

Psalm 22:4-5

Blessed are those who have had fathers, mothers, grandparents, and other ancestors who trusted in the Lord. Not all of us can claim a godly heritage, having found Christ on our own, without the benefit of a faith-filled family. But the good news is that *we* can be the start of a godly lineage. We can pass our faith on to the next generation and beyond. Either way—whether from a godly family or as a new believer in the family line—we can rejoice at our opportunities.

O Lord, today I'm thankful you have revealed yourself to me as the God who can be trusted—the God who delivers from evil.

Not all of the fathers in my lineage have known your goodness, but I do! And my prayer is for all who come after me—and for all I might influence, whether kin to me or not. Bless, O God, Christian families. May their numbers increase. May faith in you be passed along from generation to generation. Let the circle be unbroken.

Today's Takeaway

God will always have a people in future generations. May my descendants be among them!

HASTE THEE!

Be not thou far from me, O LORD: O my strength, haste thee to help me.

PSALM 22:19

In times of distress, sometimes God seems far away. We ask, "Where are you, Lord?" But *is* he far away...or is he as near as he has ever been?

Make no mistake, God is never absent from our lives. Through hard times and good times, he's always there. Neither is he too slow to respond to our cries. We ask him to hasten to our aid, forgetting that he doesn't have to rush. He's already there and he's already got a solution to our troubling situation.

As the saying goes, "Everything will be all right in the end. If it's not all right, it's not the end."

From my limited point of view, God, you often seem slow to move ahead with your will for me. This seems especially true during tough times. But I know you are never slow. It's I who am too quick to allow you to truly be Lord in my life.

Yes, I may pray for you to "haste thee," but your reply might be "chill thee."

Today's Takeaway

God is always on time, never slow, according to heavenly time.

Surely Goodness and Mercy

The Lord is my shepherd; I shall not want. He maketh me to lie down in green pastures: he leadeth me beside the still waters. He restoreth my soul: he leadeth me in the paths of righteousness for his name's sake. Yea, though I walk through the valley of the shadow of death, I will fear no evil: for thou art with me; thy rod and thy staff they comfort me. Thou preparest a table before me in the presence of mine enemies: thou anointest my head with oil; my cup runneth over. Surely goodness and mercy shall follow me all the days of my life: and I will dwell in the house of the Lord for ever.

Psalm 23:1-6

How pleasant it is to be a sheep under the watchful eye of the Good Shepherd. Today is a day to lie down in his green pastures and allow him to restore our weary soul. Here, beside the still waters, we fear no evil. Our Shepherd is here. His rod and staff comfort us. We have before us a table, prepared by our Shepherd. Our cup runneth over.

No matter how fast we think we can run, goodness and mercy are following close behind and will do so all the days of our lives. Best of all, we will dwell forever in the house of the Lord.

Father, there is no greater comfort than resting in your green pastures. I gladly follow your lead along the still waters. Praise you, Father, for the goodness and mercy you have sent after me to guard my ways. Most of all, thank you for allowing me to dwell in your heavenly house forever.

Today's Takeaway

I abide daily in God's green pastures.

THE KING OF GLORY

Lift up your heads, O ye gates; and be ye lift up,
ye everlasting doors; and the King of glory shall come in.
Who is this King of glory?
The LORD strong and mighty, the LORD mighty in battle.
PSALM 24:7-8

One of the many titles we see in the Bible to describe our God is "the King of glory." It's fitting because he *is* king—and he *is* glorious. As king, he is also our commander in battle against the wiles of the enemy. With our strong and mighty God leading the church, we are assured of victory. So lift up your heads, O ye gates; be lifted up and the King of glory shall come in! God is mighty in battle on my behalf.

You, our God, are not a weak God. You are the Lord, strong and mighty, a leader in battle. To you I lift up my head as the King of glory at the gate requesting entry. You enter as both a king and a commander in battle. You are my Lord, my strength.

What have I to fear? You have become my courage.

Today's Takeaway

Give God praise today for his strength and might in battle.
Let him come through the gates.

PARDON MINE INIQUITY

Remember not the sins of my youth, nor my transgressions: according to thy mercy remember thou me for thy goodness' sake, O LORD... For thy name's sake, O LORD, pardon mine iniquity; for it is great.

PSALM 25:7, 11

The story of the Bible is the history of sinners in need of redemption and renewed fellowship with God. We have our redemption at the cost of Christ's blood. So when we pray that God not remember our sins and transgressions, we can know that prayer is heard and is answered by a glance at the cross where Christ made it possible for the Father to remember our sins no more.

We ask God for mercy in light of his goodness and no matter how great our iniquity, God remembers it no longer—and neither should we.

O Lord, I have much to thank you for, but chief among my blessings is the total, complete, "it is finished" sacrifice for my many gross and even not-so-gross sins. All of our sins are gone forever, utterly forgiven by you because of Christ's sacrifice. If you no longer can remember my past, neither shall I. Thank you, Lord, for the blessed assurance of forgiveness.

Today's Takeaway

God remembers not the many sins of my youth.

The Secret of the Lord

The secret of the Lord is with them that fear him;
and he will show them his covenant.
Psalm 25:14

There are spiritual truths that are hidden from the lost and known only to those who have entered into covenant with God. To those who know not Christ, the idea of a savior surrendering his life for the remission of the sins of the world is foolishness. To us who believe, it is a revelation of a divine secret: the innocent paying the price of the guilty. We were availed of this secret the day we first feared God and said yes to the "new covenant," which is the gospel. Heaven is no doubt full of wonderful secrets that will one day be revealed to us.

Lord, how wise of you to hide your truths in secrecy. Only those with ears to hear and eyes to see, and faith to believe, have access to your secrets. Thank you for the covenant of grace—surely the greatest secret of all and the best of news to sinners in need of redemption. Father, I pray for a life of open secrecy in view of others so that they may be drawn to the great covenant that has set your people free.

Today's Takeaway

God's secrets are for his children to know.

HABITATION

LORD, I have loved the habitation of thy house,
and the place where thine honor dwelleth.
PSALM 26:8

The believer in Christ is constantly enthralled by the graciousness of God. We love God first and foremost, but we also love his heaven—his habitation where his honor dwells. Our Lord has issued an invitation to us to be with him there. He has put out the welcome mat. We enter to enjoy his presence and find happiness we have not known on earth. We love his habitation because he is there.

And God rejoices because we are there.

Lord, heaven will be heaven not because of pearly gates and streets of gold. No, heaven will be heaven because it is your home. And when I leave this earth, it will be at your invitation to join you in your heavenly habitation. Honor dwells there, along with purity, righteousness, and love. Your invitation is backed up by your promises to those who believe. Like the apostle Paul, I long to be there—present with Christ, absent from this mortal body. Lord, you choose the day, and I will be packed and ready!

Today's Takeaway

Heaven is heaven because God is there.

To Dwell in the House of the Lord

One thing have I desired of the LORD, that will I seek after; that I may dwell in the house of the LORD all the days of my life, to behold the beauty of the LORD, and to enquire in his temple.

PSALM 27:4

Not only are we invited into God's habitation as a guest, but we are also invited to dwell in the house of the Lord all the days of our lives. And what do we do there? Gloriously, we behold the beauty of our God—a sight we will enjoy for all eternity. We find answers there for all our questions. We finally see our loved ones who arrived before us.

When we are with God in his house, we are at home at last. Our hearts are full.

O Father, my one desire is to dwell in the house of the Lord all the days of my life. I ache to behold your beauty and to inquire in your temple. Lord, this desire, the longing of all of us who love you, is our priority. Be with us here and now, and then for all eternity in our home with you.

Today's Takeaway

Dwelling in the house of the Lord is my one desire.

Wait

Wait on the Lord: be of good courage,
and he shall strengthen thine heart: wait, I say, on the Lord.
Psalm 27:14

For most of us, waiting is hard. When we are harried by life, waiting is not our plan A (or B or C either). But in waiting we grow courage. Our faint hearts are strengthened. We have said we trust God, and now we have the opportunity (one of many!) to affirm our trust by willingly waiting for our Creator to move on our behalf.

Lord, when you created us, you knew we would be impatient for many things—often the fulfilling of our own will, with your will as a grudging second best. So considering the impatience of your human creations, you have implemented the need to wait. By waiting, we gain patience, we overcome the childish "me first, me now" syndrome. So many people in the Bible were "waiters"—Job, Abraham, Sarah, Moses, David, Hannah, and more. Lord, you gave them as examples of what happens when we wait and be of good courage. All of these and others were blessed in waiting. God, I wait for you. Strengthen my heart!

Today's Takeaway

Patience is God's way. Impatience is man's way.

O LORD, BE NOT SILENT!

Unto thee will I cry, O LORD my rock; be not silent to me: lest, if thou be silent to me, I become like them that go down into the pit. Hear the voice of my supplications, when I cry unto thee, when I lift up my hands toward thy holy oracle.

PSALM 28:1-2

When we cry out to God, we're not just talking into thin air. Our Creator is not silent. He is not passive. Our Lord is a *rock*. Without faith in such a God, we would be without hope—we'd be like those who, for lack of saving faith, go down into the pit.

Lift your hands in praise. We cry, and he hears!

Lord, I join the psalmist in crying out to you. I pray you will not be silent to my prayers, lest I be like those that go down into the pit of no return. For them, I pray for hearts to open to your redeeming love.

Yes, Father, hear the voice of my supplications. I lift my hands up to you, as in surrender. Hear my plea!

Today's Takeaway

I lift my hands and my heart to the God who hears my cry.

Save Thy People

Blessed be the Lord, because he hath heard the voice of my supplications.
The Lord is my strength and my shield; my heart trusted
in him, and I am helped: therefore my heart greatly
rejoiceth; and with my song will I praise him.
The Lord is their strength, and he is the saving strength of his anointed.
Save thy people, and bless thine inheritance: feed
them also, and lift them up for ever.

Psalm 28:6-9

It's amazing how often God's Word builds up the believer, unlike our enemy who wants to tear us down. We ask God to save us—and he does. We are, after all, his inheritance. Our Lord not only saves us, but he also feeds us from the green grass of his pasture. He hears the voice of our supplications; he lifts us up when we are down.

God's word is clear: He is *for* us in every aspect of life. We are deeply loved and cared for.

Lord, so many times I've relied on my own puny strength—and failed. Now my heart trusts in you, and I rejoice and praise you with my song. You are my saving strength, you bless me as your inheritance, you feed me and lift me up. How, then, can I fail in life?

Today's Takeaway

God is my strength and my shield.

Give Him the Glory

Give unto the Lord, *O ye mighty, give unto the* Lord *glory and strength.*
Give unto the Lord *the glory due unto his name;*
worship the Lord *in the beauty of holiness.*
Psalm 29:1-2

When we find worship less than uplifting—or worse, boring—we need a renewal of our attitude. Giving God glory in worship is simply *due* him. We need only to recount the many times he has come to our rescue to bring us back to our knees. Our worship need not be loud or even emotional—but it must be real. A revelation of the beauty of his holiness and a contemplation of our holiness (found in Christ) will surely fuel renewed worship coming straight from our hearts.

Father, you are worthy of all praise. I give you the glory due unto your name. I worship you in the beauty of holiness. May my adoration of you never grow old. May it never be passive or merely a recitation of words that don't come from my heart. Lord, may you constantly renew my desire to praise you in all things and at all times.

Today's Takeaway

I give God the glory due his name.

Strength and Peace

The Lord will give strength unto his people; the Lord will bless his people with peace.
Psalm 29:11

God has a multitude of gifts to give to his children…gifts without number. One of the most desirable gifts is *strength*. This is not ordinary human strength—this is godly strength given to us so we can overcome the obstacles we face in life.

Another wonderful gift is *peace*. As with strength, this isn't ordinary human peace. This is that ineffable peace from God that the apostle Paul would tell us surpasses all human understanding. It guards our minds, settles our souls, and gives us confidence in prayer.

All of God's gifts are received by faith. Pray today believing in God's promised gifts of strength and peace, and you shall have them. To neglect God's gifts is to reject God's gifts.

Lord, I have many needs. But two of the most urgent are strength and peace. I ask you for strength beyond myself and peace that passes understanding. As these are promised gifts, I will receive them by faith and renew their presence daily.

Today's Takeaway

I receive God's gifts of strength and peace by faith.

MORNING JOY

O LORD my God, I cried unto thee, and thou hast healed me...
His anger endureth but a moment; in his favor is life:
weeping may endure for a night, but joy cometh in the morning.
PSALM 30:2, 5

We have all had our nights of weeping—perhaps many. But such times come to pass, not to stay. Morning eventually comes, bringing joy with the sunrise. This is the way of life for the Christian—understanding that God's anger is momentary, but the joys of morning are everlasting. If you are currently weeping in the night, God would have you look up and say, "Yes, Lord. I can wait until you bring the morning and its joy."

When we need healing, we cry to God and receive the blessing of his touch.

Father, I've shed tears in the night but awakened to joy in the morning. Other times, I've awakened not to gladness and rejoicing but to the same troubling situation from the night before. Help me learn to look for and accept morning joy, even when my situation doesn't change. Help me remember that in your favor is life, that in your presence is healing.
In that I can surely rejoice.

Today's Takeaway

Though weeping has a beginning, it also has an end. Joy is the result.

Mourning into Dancing

Thou hast turned for me my mourning into
dancing: thou hast put off my sackcloth,
and girded me with gladness; to the end that my glory
may sing praise to thee, and not be silent.
O Lord my God, I will give thanks unto thee for ever.
Psalm 30:11-12

Are we in mourning? If not, we at some point will be. Grieving and loss are part of our lot in this life. But as Christians, in due time our mourning becomes dancing. The sackcloth is put off, and we find ourselves girded with gladness. What, then, is the result? Praises! How can one be silent when the sackcloth has been replaced by joy?

Give thanks today. The sackcloth is coming off. Gladness awaits. Praise and thanks are in order.

Father, today is a day of gladness, praise, and thanks—no matter what the day holds. I resolve to put off my sackcloth of worry, sadness, and anxiety. That garment is worn out! Now I put on the garments of praise. I will give thanks to thee today and forever, for you, Lord, have turned my mourning into dancing.

Today's Takeaway

God turns my mourning into dancing…in his time.

Be of Good Courage

O love the Lord, all ye his saints: for the Lord preserveth the faithful, and plentifully rewardeth the proud doer.
Be of good courage, and he shall strengthen your heart, all ye that hope in the Lord.

Psalm 31:23-24

Loving the Lord is not hard. He who made us watches over us. He preserves us through every trial, and as we face life with courage, he strengthens us day by day. We hope in him because we know him—and love him.

Father, it is so easy to love you, for you preserve us, your saints—your sanctified ones, set apart for your purposes. You keep us in every circumstance. You enable me to stand full of good courage with a strengthened heart. It is thus easy to also hope in you. Nothing can come across my path that courage, strength, and hope can't overcome. I am victorious in you!

Today's Takeaway

I am set aside for God's use. He preserves me.

I Will Guide Thee

I will instruct thee and teach thee in the way which thou shalt go:
I will guide thee with mine eye.
Be ye not as the horse, or as the mule, which have no understanding: whose mouth must be held in with bit and bridle, lest they come near unto thee.
Many sorrows shall be to the wicked: but he that trusteth in the LORD, mercy shall compass him about.
Be glad in the LORD, and rejoice, ye righteous: and shout for joy, all ye that are upright in heart.

PSALM 32:8-11

Why do we often wander off the right trail in life, somehow attracted to the wrong path? God's remedy is for us not to trust our own natural eyes but to rely on his eye. God knows our foreordained path, and he knows where we need to go next.

Never fear new beginnings if God has instructed you in the way you should go. His clear eye sees what is hidden from us. Goodness awaits us when we trust his leadership.

God, my eyes are weak and can't clearly discern the path you have for me. Show me the way I should go each day. Instruct me through your Word and guide me with your clear eye.

For your guidance, I rejoice and shout for joy. I love your mercy that compasses me about. I feel safe under your watchful eye.

Today's Takeaway

I have no fear of taking the wrong path. God guides my way.

His Eye Is Upon Us

He loveth righteousness and judgment: the earth is full of the goodness of the LORD...
The LORD bringeth the counsel of the heathen to nought: he maketh the devices of the people of none effect. The counsel of the LORD standeth for ever, the thoughts of his heart to all generations.

PSALM 33:5, 10-11

When we compare the counsel of the world to the counsel of the Lord, we easily find that the former is changeable, depending on whatever current "counsel" is in vogue. But in the latter—in God's counsel—we find that it is permanent, not subject to earthly whims. Wise is the Christian who abandons the counsel of the heathen and trusts in the guidance of the Lord. His thoughts will remain steadfast and true through all generations.

Lord, you love righteousness and true judgment. The earth is full of your goodness. I need only to look and see it through pure eyes. I refuse to consider the counsel of the world when it contradicts your counsel, Lord. Your guidance stands forever; it extends to all generations.

Today's Takeaway

God is my counselor in every situation.

Taste and See!

The angel of the Lord encampeth round about
them that fear him, and delivereth them.
O taste and see that the Lord is good: blessed
is the man that trusteth in him.

Psalm 34:7-8

God invites us to taste and see that he is good. In essence, he's offering us a free trial, knowing that having once tasted his goodness, we will not look elsewhere for happiness. In him, we trust and, as promised, we find blessing upon blessing. The taste of the enemy goes down sweet but returns bitter. Not so with our Lord. He blesses us in all ways and sends his angels to encamp around us, protecting us, delivering us.

Lord, I have tasted what the world has to offer and found it wanting. But you are different, Father. The taste of your love is sweet and lasting. It doesn't have the bitter aftertaste of the world's wisdom. In you I find blessing. I know there are angels encamped around me to guard me and to deliver me from evil. Praise you, Lord, for every heavenly blessing.

Today's Takeaway

I trust in God; therefore, I am blessed!

We Shall Not Want

O fear the LORD, ye his saints: for there is no want to them that fear him.
The young lions do lack, and suffer hunger:
but they that seek the LORD shall not want any good thing.

Psalm 34:9-10

What is it you need? If it is a "good thing," you will have it if you seek after the Lord.

Others may hunger and partake of the world's offering, but they soon return hungry again. God sees to it that his children are fed from the fat of the land and are satisfied. Turn your wants into prayers of thanksgiving. You will have the good things that you need. What you will not have is what you do not need.

Fearing you, Lord, brings many blessings, including a life not lacking in the good things I need. Yes, the young lions may lack and suffer hunger, but as I seek you and fear you, I shall not want any good thing. Anything I don't have, I either do not need or, if I need it, it's on the way to me.

Today's Takeaway

With God as my provider, I lack nothing.

THE LORD OF THE BROKENHEARTED

The LORD is nigh unto them that are of a broken heart;
and saveth such as be of a contrite spirit.
Many are the afflictions of the righteous: but the
LORD delivereth him out of them all.
PSALM 34:18-19

God loves broken people. He witnesses their plight; he hears their prayers. He looks back into the past and sees the causes of their brokenness. He acknowledges the contrite spirit that speaks through tears. When we are broken, he is the nearest. When we are of a contrite spirit, he saves us. And though our afflictions are many, he sees the cause, and he arranges the coming end of them to work in our best interests.

Lord, it seems you are nearest to us when our hearts are breaking. And you, Father, know the pain of a wounded heart, for you watched your Son crucified by your enemies. Yet your love remains fixed on your foes—as you instruct us to do with ours. You see my many afflictions, Lord, and you promise to deliver me from them all. I praise you, my deliverer.

Today's Takeaway

God sees me best in my brokenness.

Magnify the Lord

Let them shout for joy, and be glad, that favor my righteous cause: yea, let them say continually, Let the LORD be magnified, which hath pleasure in the prosperity of his servant. And my tongue shall speak of thy righteousness and of thy praise all the day long.

Psalm 35:27-28

God is worthy of our shouts of joy. He is always to be magnified, praised, and exalted in our lives. Our lips must show forth his praise continually. When he prospers us in our endeavors, he is pleasured to be our source of all prosperity. Have we any good thing that didn't come from the Lord? No, all is from him: past blessings, present provision, and future abundance. For that reason, we shall praise him all day long.

God, you take pleasure when I prosper. But in reality, I prosper because you take delight in me. It's thus easy to be glad in your presence and to shout for joy. May you forever be magnified. Today my tongue shall praise you all day long. May my prosperity continue as your blessings flow toward me.

Today's Takeaway

Because God has pleasure in my prosperity, I shout for joy.

The Shadow of His Wings

How excellent is thy lovingkindness, O God!
Therefore the children of men put their trust under the shadow of thy wings. They shall be abundantly satisfied with the fatness of thy house; and thou shalt make them drink of the river of thy pleasures.
Psalm 36:7-8

God's loving-kindness can be fully trusted, if not fully grasped. Our heavenly Father welcomes us to hide ourselves under the protective shadow of his wings. Danger may surround us, but when we flee to God and experience his loving-kindness, we find the shadow of his wings shelters us from the storms outside. How excellent is his loving-kindness! With God, we shall be abundantly satisfied. We shall drink from the river of pleasures.

Lord, I love the word abundantly! That's how you satisfy me. You offer me divine protection under your wings, and then you promise satisfaction from the fatness of your house—and refreshment from the river of your pleasures. O God, it is too much for me! And yet I receive it with praise and thanksgiving. How excellent is your loving-kindness!

Today's Takeaway

Because of God's loving-kindness, he gives to me abundantly.

In Thy Light

For with thee is the fountain of life: in thy light shall we see light. O continue thy lovingkindness unto them that know thee; and thy righteousness to the upright in heart. Let not the foot of pride come against me, and let not the hand of the wicked remove me.

Psalm 36:9-11

In God, we have both light and the fountain of life. With no fountain, there is no true life—only death. With no light, there is only darkness. And in darkness, we can see nothing. We are blind. Darkness is the absence of light. Light, on the other hand, enables us to see clearly, to discern our path, to walk ahead confidently. God's light shines bright on our path.

Pride will be our downfall if we ever think our blessings come from ourselves. Our prayer, then, is always to remain humble and trust God for protection from the hand of the wicked.

Thank you, Father, for your light and your fountain of life. May your loving-kindness continue to flow toward me. May the righteousness of Christ always be the source of acceptance with you. Keep me from the many dangers of arrogant pride, and I pray you will not allow the wicked hand of the enemy to remove me from your perfect will.

Today's Takeaway

With God is the fountain of life.

Delighting in the Lord

Delight thyself also in the LORD: and he shall give thee the desires of thine heart. Commit thy way unto the LORD; trust also in him; and he shall bring it to pass.

Psalm 37:4-5

In what do we delight? There are so many options. But none can compare with delighting in the Lord. Not only is such joy its own reward, but we are also promised the desires of our heart.

Delighting in the Lord means that we commit all our ways to him, that we trust him to bring to pass those heartfelt desires. It means loving God above all else.

Maybe it's time for an inventory of delights. Is the Lord your number one delight? If not, edit your priority list.

Father, I do delight in you. Ironically, I know you also delight in me. What a blessing. What a miracle! You know the desires of my heart better than I do, so I commit them all to you, just as I also commit all my ways to you, trusting you to bring to pass a life of delights.

Today's Takeaway

God will give me the desires of my heart because I delight in him.

My Steps Are Ordered by the Lord

The steps of a good man are ordered by the
Lord: and he delighteth in his way.
Though he fall, he shall not be utterly cast down: for
the Lord upholdeth him with his hand.
Psalm 37:23-24

What on earth could I possibly fear when my steps are ordered by God? Further, the Lord delights in those steps. Yes, I may fall now and then, but even so, I will not be utterly cast down, because God upholds me. I am quickly back on my feet and walking in my Creator's ordered steps. No, I fear nothing...but God.

Lord, if I am a "good" person, it's because you are good. You are ordering my steps every day. Each year that passes has your footprints on it, as you have walked with me through the days, both good and bad. When I have been cast down, you've been there to pick me up. When I fall, I am not utterly destroyed, for you uphold me with your hand. Thank you, Father, for delighting in my way, just as I delight in your ways.

Today's Takeaway

If I should fall, the Lord will lift me up again.

THE BLESSED BURDEN OF MY INIQUITY

For mine iniquities are gone over mine head: as an heavy burden they are too heavy for me.
PSALM 38:4

It may sound strange to think of our iniquity as a blessed burden. To be sure, iniquity is a deadly poison that we must avoid. But when the burden of our iniquity is so heavy that it drives us to our great sin bearer, Jesus, it becomes a blessing. The burden of sin can have one of two results. We either run from God or run to him. Let it always be the latter.

Dear Lord, I remember that when Adam and Eve sinned, they hid themselves from you. When I sin, my desire is to run to you. I confess my failings, repent, and claim by faith your forgiveness. Yes, I have learned that there's no other way of dealing with my sin. I can't make it go away by performing good works or by any ritualistic repetitions. There is only one remedy: reliance on the cleansing blood of Christ to take away the stain.

Sin is a burden, Lord. But it's the burden that sends me running to you for restoration.

Today's Takeaway

Sin drives me to my great sin bearer.

All My Desire Is Before Thee

I am troubled; I am bowed down greatly; I go mourning all the day long.
For my loins are filled with a loathsome disease:
and there is no soundness in my flesh.
I am feeble and sore broken: I have roared by
reason of the disquietness of my heart.
Lord, all my desire is before thee; and my groaning is not hid from thee.
My heart panteth, my strength faileth me: as for the
light of mine eyes, it also is gone from me.
Psalm 38:6-10

David was as low as he could go. He was so far down that the light of his eyes was gone, his strength was gone, and his prayers were but groans. And yet David still maintained that all his desire was before God. Though he had seemingly given up hope, there remained his panting heart. All his desire stayed before God. Where else could he turn?

When we're troubled, bowed down, or full of mourning, we must summon up that last crumb of hope—perhaps the size of a mustard seed—and trust in God.

He will see us through. Just ask David.

Father of lights, like David, I've been brought low both by adversity and by my own foolishness. Like David, I'm feeble and sore broken. O God, hear my groans. Come to my aid and lift me up again. I pant for your presence. Restore the joyful glow to my eyes. Come, Lord, come!

Today's Takeaway

David was brought low, but God was there. David's God is my God.

My Frailty

Lord, make me to know mine end, and the measure of my days, what it is: that I may know how frail I am. Behold, thou hast made my days as an handbreadth; and mine age is as nothing before thee: verily every man at his best state is altogether vanity.

Psalm 39:4-5

We are on this planet for a very short time. God alone knows the measure of our days. We know only our frailty and how far we fall short of our Creator's glory. Though that's how we see ourselves, we must remind ourselves of God's deep love for we who are so frail and at our best state, altogether vanity.

God, surely wisdom is knowing how fleeting this life is. Indeed, my years on earth are short. Short and frail. Yet you have given me my years as a gift. Teach me to use my time here wisely. Let me not be wasteful of the days, nor negligent of the gifts for service you've deposited in me. If possible, Lord, extend my time here. Give me more days and years to fully accomplish my divine assignments.

Today's Takeaway

My years on earth are few. I will make the most of them.

Thy Wonderful Works

Many, O Lord my God, are thy wonderful works which thou hast done, and thy thoughts which are to us-ward: they cannot be reckoned up in order unto thee: if I would declare and speak of them, they are more than can be numbered.

Psalm 40:5

Pondering the Lord and his mighty works is an awesome pastime. But even greater is to consider that his thoughts (God's thoughts!) are focused on us. Thoughts without number. Thoughts of blessings. Thoughts of divine love. When we thus ponder, we are at once brought low with humility and yet boosted in worth to consider how important we are in God's plan. His eyes are always upon us, his thoughts toward us.

Father, words fail me. Wonderful are your many works. I'm awestruck by your creativity. It's incredible that you have given each of us a life here on earth and made yourself knowable to us. Your thoughts are always of us, and your goodness pursues us to bring us blessings. You are indebted to no one—we are all indebted to you and are thankful.

Today's Takeaway

God does mighty works, many of which are in my life.

Consider the Poor

Blessed is he that considereth the poor: the LORD will deliver him in time of trouble. The LORD will preserve him, and keep him alive; and he shall be blessed upon the earth: and thou wilt not deliver him unto the will of his enemies. The LORD will strengthen him upon the bed of languishing: thou wilt make all his bed in his sickness.

PSALM 41:1-3

God loves the poor. And he expects to bless the poor through the wallets of his prosperous children. To be well-off in this life and neglect God's poor is to act in contradiction to his promise of blessing to those who consider the poor. High on our list of spiritual priorities should be our duty to the impoverished. We then have the promise of deliverance in time of trouble.

O Lord, you have blessed me at times with little and then again with much. In all seasons, I remember the poor. I remember the widow whom Jesus commended for giving out of her own poverty, while others gave out of their excess. Father, the poor are on my mind today. Nudge me always to be a giver first and a counter of my money later. May I give as you give: lavishly.

Today's Takeaway

Because the poor are on God's heart, they are on mine.

My Soul Pants for Thee, O God

As the hart panteth after the water brooks, so panteth my soul after thee, O God. My soul thirsteth for God, for the living God: when shall I come and appear before God?

Psalm 42:1-2

There are many glitzy attractions in this world that flirt with our attention. But though their promise is great, their delivery is shallow. The glamour that draws us quickly morphs into a dark cloud of disappointment.

Not so with our attraction to God. When our soul pants after God, when we approach the living waters as does the thirsty hart, we are more than satisfied. The living God is the God of living waters.

A valid prayer is always that our soul would forever long after God.

Father, I'm so done with the gaudiness of this world. You have created a thirst in me that only you can satisfy. Lead me to your water brooks, past the desert sands of this world. Draw me, Lord. For I am like the panting hart, desiring your presence. My soul thirsts for you, the living God.

Today's Takeaway

Daily my soul yearns for God.

I Shall Yet Praise Him

Why art thou cast down, O my soul? and why art thou disquieted within me? hope in God: for I shall yet praise him, who is the health of my countenance, and my God.

Psalm 43:5

Is there now or has there ever been a Christian who has not known occasional depression? Perhaps even deep depression. David certainly did. He knew the highs and the lows of life's experiences. But David also knew where to turn during the low points. He knew that such times called for a determined instruction to his inner man to hope in God. He knew that praising God brought a fresh health to his soul, even to the affecting of his countenance.

If you are low today, speak praise to the Lord—and speak also to your downcast soul. Instruct your inner man or woman to hope in God. There is no other spiritual remedy.

God, sometimes I find myself in a pit of depression. My soul is cast down. At such times, I must hope in you. I must praise you despite the way I feel. You, Lord, are the health of my countenance. You are my God and my way out of depression's pit.

Today's Takeaway

God restores my joy when I am low.

I Trust in God

I will not trust in my bow, neither shall my sword save me.
But thou hast saved us from our enemies, and
hast put them to shame that hated us.
Psalm 44:6-7

During hard times, in our humanity, we often turn first to the carnal tools and weapons available to us. We regularly forget that tough times are allotted to us precisely to cause us to turn first and last to the Lord and his resources. Our bows and arrows fail us. Our swords are dull for the battle. God alone can save us from whatever strategies our enemies have launched to cause us to fail.

So set down your bow. Sheath your dull sword. Trust in God to save you. If you need weapons, he will furnish them.

God, I will not trust in earthly weapons to defeat my enemies. I lay aside all the useless "bows" and "swords" I've counted on in the past. Instead, I rely on you to bring my enemies to their knees. In and through you, I rise up as a victorious warrior, but to you alone belong the laurel wreaths of victory.

Today's Takeaway

My victory comes through the Lord, not my own efforts.

Endless Praise

I will make thy name to be remembered in all generations:
therefore shall the people praise thee for ever and ever.
Psalm 45:17

Doesn't an eternity of endless praise to God excite you? His name, his nature, and his love are without end—and are disbursed fresh to each new generation. God is not old. He is the same forever and is forever current.

Your generation shall praise him, but so shall the next, and the next after that. Can we thus say with David, "I will make thy name to be remembered in all generations"? Can we not pray for believers who will follow us? Can we not plead with God for future revival, ushering many more into the kingdom?

Father in heaven, you are eternally Lord of all time and all creation. There will be no end to your praises. Forever the hallelujahs shall ring.

Today's Takeaway

"When we've been there ten thousand years,
Bright shining as the sun,
We've no less days to sing God's praise
Than when we first begun."

—John Newton

Be Still, My Soul

God is our refuge and strength, a very present help in trouble.
Therefore will not we fear, though the earth be removed, and
though the mountains be carried into the midst of the sea;
though the waters thereof roar and be troubled, though
the mountains shake with the swelling thereof...
Be still, and know that I am God.

Psalm 46:1-3, 10

Rare is the soul that patiently endures stillness, especially during times of upheaval. For many of us, our soul clamors throughout the day as if to say, "Take notice of me." But God would quiet our noisy soul if we would just let him. He tells each of us as the noise reverberates in our soul, "Shh. Be still. Know that I am here. I am your God who speaks to you in quietness and calms your soul."

Listen for his still, small voice. Allow him to quiet the clamor. Especially when the mountains shake and the waters roar—even then we can be still in the midst of tumult.

O Lord, my soul seems to clamor for noise—and there is often noise around me. But in my inner being, I crave the stillness that makes room for your Spirit. In quietness, I find my faith stronger than when I'm in the midst of worldly commotion. Speak to me today, Lord, as I sit before you in silence.

Today's Takeaway

I will quiet my anxious soul and enjoy the presence of the Lord.

Sing Praises

Sing praises to God, sing praises: sing praises unto our King, sing praises. For God is the King of all the earth: sing ye praises with understanding.
Psalm 47:6-7

Would you add more joy to your life if you could? Then sing praises to God. Raise your voice and worship your Lord. Know that he is King of all the earth. He thus rules over every circumstance in your life. Nothing can befall you that praise will not overcome. Indeed, worship lays the pathway for victory. Therefore, sing praise with understanding.

Lord, I love to pray. But praying as I sing your praises is even better. Through worship, I become aware of your greatness. I experience the joy that comes with high praise. Exalting you, magnifying you comes naturally as I lift my voice in song.

You, God, are King of all the earth and worthy of praises sung and spoken. Today I sing of your greatness. Today, I receive the joy that comes with worship and adoration.

Today's Takeaway

I sing praises to my God throughout my day.

God Is Our Guide

Great is the Lord, and greatly to be praised in the city of our God, in the mountain of his holiness… This God is our God for ever and ever: he will be our guide even unto death.

Psalm 48:1, 14

We serve a great God who is eternal—a God greatly to be praised. He knew us before we were born, and he will be with us as our guide throughout our earthly sojourn. He will guide us on the right path, and should we find ourselves lost in the woods due to following our own errant desires, he will rescue us and set us back on the path he has chosen for us. He will be our sure guide even through our final days on earth. We shall pass from this earthly kingdom and awake in the presence of the One whom we have praised.

Father, we all need a guide through this life. Amidst heartache and sorrow, we need assurance that all will turn out well. And even during good times, we need a God to whom we can direct our thanks. That God is you, O Lord. You are my guide now and will be so even unto my death. In heaven, you will still be my God—and my praises will echo through eternity.

Today's Takeaway

My God is great and greatly to be praised.

THE GRAVE HAS NO POWER OVER ME

God will redeem my soul from the power of the grave: for he shall receive me.
PSALM 49:15

Yes, the grave has power. In the grave we are separated from life, gone from all we've known. Ah, but there's more for the believer in Christ: God has redeemed us from that dark power of death. He sweeps us up in his arms, receiving us with the impartation of life beyond the grave.

We need not wait until death to know this redemption. We can know it today, by faith—faith that conquers even the grave.

Lord, some people fear death—and without faith, rightly so. But because Jesus has overcome death—what the apostle Paul called the last enemy—I do not fear the grave. My body may rest there, but I will have left that mortal tent for a better incorruptible body. The power of the grave is broken forever for the one who believes in Christ. Father, I await that glorious day with anticipation. Come soon for me, Lord!

Today's Takeaway

I have no fear of death. It will usher me into God's presence.

IN THE DAY OF TROUBLE

Call upon me in the day of trouble: I will deliver thee, and thou shalt glorify me... Whoso offereth praise glorifieth me: and to him that ordereth his conversation aright will I show the salvation of God.

PSALM 50:15, 23

Trouble comes into every life, both of the believer and the unbeliever. The advantage for the one who knows and trusts in God is that we can call upon our Lord to deliver us from our trouble. Yes, God has made that promise to us—a promise he cannot break. The result is an answer to our trouble and yet another occasion to glorify our faithful Creator.

As we offer praise, we glorify God. As we order our conversation—our way of life—aright, we will see God's provision for our salvation.

Lord, I glorify you for who you are. But I also praise your name for your presence in the day of trouble. One thing I have learned, Father, is that for every trouble I face, you have the perfect solution. By prayer, faith, and counsel, I'm able to discover your solution. So yes, Lord, I do call upon you in the day of trouble. I also order my life according to your Word. In the Bible is the blueprint for a successful Christian life. Give me more understanding, O God, and I will obey your Word.

Today's Takeaway

In the day of trouble, I call upon the Lord.

Have Mercy upon Me

Have mercy upon me, O God, according to thy lovingkindness: according unto the multitude of thy tender mercies blot out my transgressions. Wash me throughly from mine iniquity, and cleanse me from my sin. For I acknowledge my transgressions: and my sin is ever before me. Against thee, thee only, have I sinned, and done this evil in thy sight: that thou mightest be justified when thou speakest, and be clear when thou judgest.

Psalm 51:1-4

It is the loving-kindness that brings forth the tender mercies of God that blot out our transgressions. In Christ, we are thoroughly clean from all our iniquity. Truthfully, our sins may seem small to us, but even the slightest transgression is an abomination to God. It's only because of Christ that our "large" and "small" sins have all been atoned for. Thus we are not the ones to judge our wrongdoings anymore. They have all been judged on the cross of Christ.

Father, I thank you for the loving-kindness and tender mercies that cleanse me from my sins, both large and small. To be sure, I know my sins and acknowledge them fully. They are grievous to me and are ever before me. But so is your forgiveness in Christ. Whether my sins are "mountainish" or anthills, all are under your tender mercy. Lord, I praise you for total forgiveness of all sin.

Today's Takeaway

I am a recipient of God's tender mercies.

Restored Joy

Restore unto me the joy of thy salvation;
and uphold me with thy free spirit.
Psalm 51:12

We experience great joy the moment of our salvation. But for many believers, that joy ebbs eventually, giving way to an unfulfilling complacency. At that point, our prayer must be like David's, asking God to restore our lost joy.

For, after all, the joy of the Lord is our strength. No joy equals no power for the abundant life. We also, like David, ask God to uphold us with his spirit—a spirit that never knows defeat nor is in want of gladness.

God is not put off when we lack the joy of our salvation, but he delights when we pray for a restoration of joy. He longs to uphold us with his Spirit.

Father, you are the fountain of joy. And just as I received joy when I first knew you, so now I pray for a restoration of that full joy. May great springs of gladness flow from your Holy Spirit, refreshing my spirit. In this joy, uphold me with your Spirit. Keep my heart fixed on the joy of salvation.

Today's Takeaway

The joy of my salvation is refreshed every day.

My Mouth Shall Praise Thee

O Lord, open thou my lips; and my mouth shall show forth thy praise.
For thou desirest not sacrifice; else would I give
it: thou delightest not in burnt offering.
The sacrifices of God are a broken spirit: a broken and
a contrite heart, O God, thou wilt not despise.
Psalm 51:15-17

The mouth of the believer in Christ is compelled to show forth God's praises. It's what we were made for, why we continue to live. It's as simple as God desiring a family of praisers.

The irony is that in worshipping God, we benefit the most. Praise fills a space in our hearts that results in the Lord opening our lips to show forth his praise. Praising God is the most natural instinct of the Christian. Worship him now and reap the blessings.

Father, I surrender my lips to you to show forth your praise. Though many people may offer you a sacrifice of their choosing, I know that the only sacrifice you receive is a broken spirit and a contrite heart. These, Lord, I do offer upon your altar today.

Today's Takeaway

My mouth speaks the praises of God.

God's Olive Tree

I am like a green olive tree in the house of God:
I trust in the mercy of God for ever and ever. I will praise
thee for ever, because thou hast done it: and I will wait
on thy name; for it is good before thy saints.

Psalm 52:8-9

We are God's tender plants—his well-cared-for olive trees. We are not like the dry, water-forsaken cactus, alone in a desert. We are in the house of God where our heavenly Father is able to watch over us daily, watering us, feeding us, exposing us to the sun's warm rays. We are sheltered from the storms outside, trusting in the mercy of our Lord forever. Thus do we praise him forever and rejoice in his deeds for our good.

Father, I am fully yours. I am like your green olive tree set apart in your heavenly greenhouse. There you care for me. You water me, feed me, and make sure I partake of your radiant light. The goal, Lord, is for me to be a fruitful olive tree in your house. This, dear Father, is my purpose. Therefore, I continually praise you and wait on your name. Blessed are you, O Lord!

Today's Takeaway

God cares for me like a master gardener
watches over his tender plants.

No, Not One

God looked down from heaven upon the children of men, to see if there were any that did understand, that did seek God. Every one of them is gone back: they are altogether become filthy; there is none that doeth good, no, not one.

Psalm 53:2-3

Sometimes we look around us and judge that people aren't really so bad. Other times, we look around and wonder why God hasn't brought down the final curtain on mankind. The truth is that despite the corruption of man through Adam's sin, carried on down through the generations and eventually reaching us, God redeems us though we have become altogether filthy. There is none that doeth good. No, not one.

God, if you ask who has sinned, I must raise my hand. You already know my standing as a sinner. I'm part of humanity, thus I fail in doing good. But wait. That's not the end of it. Because of Christ, I'm now numbered among your saints. Forgiveness is mine along with all the other gifts set aside for your believers. I praise you, Lord, that you didn't leave us in our sinful state.

Today's Takeaway

Though I was once counted among the sinners,
now I'm numbered among the saints.

The Goodness of Praise

I will freely sacrifice unto thee:
I will praise thy name, O Lord*; for it is good. For he hath delivered me out of all trouble: and mine eye hath seen his desire upon mine enemies.*
Psalm 54:6-7

We are under no compulsion to praise the Lord, but we do so freely because our Creator is the victorious God who has delivered us from all trouble. We have no other sacrifice suitable for our Lord, except praise. And yet that is the only sacrifice God asks of us. And that sacrifice issues from our hearts full of praise and worship. God is good—very good—and thus it's with ease that we offer the sacrifice of praise.

God, freely do I praise you. I'm under no compulsion to do so. I could choose not to offer the sacrifice of praise...but that would be foolish in the extreme. For all I have comes from you. My salvation, sanctification, spiritual gifts, my future heavenly home—all that and more come from your generous hand. How, then, can I not praise your name?

Today's Takeaway

I freely offer the sacrifice of praise to my God and King.

Sustain Me, O Lord

As for me, I will call upon God; and the Lord shall save me.
Evening, and morning, and at noon, will I pray,
and cry aloud: and he shall hear my voice…
Cast thy burden upon the Lord, and he shall sustain thee:
he shall never suffer the righteous to be moved.
Psalm 55:16-17, 22

Our God is a rock! When we feel like we're sinking in the quicksand of adversity, we must gather the strength to reach out to the hand of the Lord as he sets us on his firm ground. We call on him relentlessly, morning, noon, and night. Our pleas are thus heard in heaven at all times.

It is during these storms of life that we can and must cry aloud in our distress, that we must cast the present burden upon the Lord and allow him to sustain us. In him, we are strong. In him is safety. He will not allow us to be moved.

Lord, in the storms of life, I often feel shaken by the fierce winds. But you, Father, are my rock. When I stand on you, I cannot be moved. I laugh at the hurricanes of life, knowing that until they pass, I'm immovable. My prayers are endless and reach your ears as I cry out every morning, noon, and night.

Today's Takeaway

God sustains me in all of life's events.

You Have Bottled My Tears

Thou tellest my wanderings: put thou my tears into thy bottle: are they not in thy book?
Psalm 56:8

Our tears are never lost. God hears our laments; he follows us as we wander; he records our losses. Every tear is put in the bottle with our name on it. And every grief we've known will be redeemed. Loss is gain when we live by faith. Crying is not a sin. Weep openly—fill the bottle.

Lord, I have laughed, and I have cried. During the time of weeping, you have collected my every tear in a bottle with my name on it. Surely by now there must be at least a second bottle. It makes the sadness lighter to know how close you are during the hard times.

Yes, some tears have come from my wandering. Other tears fell due to circumstances beyond my control. Lord, no matter the cause, save those bottled tears. They will remind me of all the times you comforted me and dried my eyes.

Today's Takeaway

God takes special notice of my tears. He collects them in his bottle.

A Fixed Heart

My heart is fixed, O God, my heart is fixed: I will sing and give praise...Be thou exalted, O God, above the heavens: let thy glory be above all the earth.

Psalm 57:7, 11

Are our hearts fixed on God? Or are our hearts divided between our God and our attractions? The latter are designed to woo us away from the former. Happiness is the result of a heart fixed on the Lord, no matter the circumstances, no matter the tempting attractions.

A fixed heart can sing the songs of joy. It can give praise when passing through deep valleys. It can exalt God above the heavens and his glory above all the earth.

Fix your heart on God and sing his praises.

Lord, there are so many distractions in my life that threaten to move me away from you. But by an act of faith, I deny those temptations and decidedly fix my heart on you. Therefore, I will sing and give praise. I exalt you, O God. Let your glory be above all the earth.

Today's Takeaway

A fixed heart will not be moved by earthly distractions.

A Reward for the Righteous

A man shall say, Verily there is a reward for the righteous:
verily he is a God that judgeth in the earth.

Psalm 58:11

We are not righteous by faith in order to receive a reward from God. Our imputed righteousness (the righteousness of Christ) is its own reward. And yet God has determined that righteousness by faith is to be rewarded. That is the graciousness and generosity of our Lord.

God is our judge, and he has issued a decree in our favor. Not only does the judge pronounce us "not guilty," but he also extends a reward in our favor. Both the verdict and the reward are ours only because of Christ. They are never based on our own merits.

That being the case, we should take pleasure in our coming reward.

O Lord, that you should judge me as righteous because of my faith in Christ is a wonder in itself. But to be rewarded for righteousness is like dessert after a fine meal. O God, I do not deserve the righteousness you have imputed to me. Neither do I deserve my coming reward. It will be reward enough just to dwell in your presence eternally.

Today's Takeaway

There is a reward awaiting the righteous.

I Will Sing Aloud

I will sing of thy power; yea, I will sing aloud
of thy mercy in the morning:
for thou hast been my defense and refuge in the day of my trouble.
Unto thee, O my strength, will I sing: for God is
my defense, and the God of my mercy.
Psalm 59:16-17

Do we need power in our lives? Then let us sing of *his* power available to us. Do we need mercy? Do we need a defender? All of these and more await us each morning. We need only to receive them by faith. Even during days of trouble, his power remains with us. It never leaves. He is our defense and refuge in all circumstances. He is our God of great mercies.

Yes, Lord, I will sing of your power and of your mercies, fresh every morning. I will take refuge in you in the day of trouble, for you are my defense. Yes, unto you, O my Strength, will I sing! Yes, and I will boast in your goodness to me.

Today's Takeaway

I will sing praise to the God of all power.

We Shall Do Valiantly

Give us help from trouble: for vain is the help of man.
Through God we shall do valiantly: for he it is
that shall tread down our enemies.
Psalm 60:11-12

Who among us does not want to "do valiantly"? We all wish to triumph over our enemies, but when we go up against our foes, we fail to conquer them with our meager strength and our insufficient resources. Here, though, we read the secret of victory: It is *through God* that we shall do valiantly.

Surrender your own power and take up his strength. Set aside your failing resources and allow God to formulate a plan. Then will the enemies fall. Do not trust in the vain help of man.

Father God, save me from all trouble. You are my hope because the help of man is vain. Only through you do I prevail against my enemies. Infuse me with power. Restore my confidence in victory when trouble arises. Give me your resources to wage a winning war against the enemy of my soul.

Today's Takeaway

Through God I shall do valiantly.

I Have a Heritage

From the end of the earth will I cry unto thee, when my heart is overwhelmed: lead me to the rock that is higher than I…
Thou, O God, hast heard my vows: thou hast given me the heritage of those that fear thy name.

Psalm 61:2, 5

God knows no distance. We may cry out to him from the ends of the earth or from our living room recliner and he hears us and leads to the rock high above the troubling waters below.

Among our many blessings as children of God, we are given a heritage. And like all heritages, it is valuable—a veritable treasure.

It seems some of that heritage is for our present life—David, after all, enjoyed much of his heritage while he walked this earth. And yet he also knew much earthly sorrow. Thus we can assume that in eternity David's full heritage—and ours—will be manifest.

Lord, when my heart is overwhelmed, I cry to you for help. Take me to the rock that is higher than the stormy water below. Give me, Father, the heritage of those who fear your name.

Today's Takeaway

My vows to God are heard and received. I shall have a true heritage.

I Will Pour Out My Heart

My soul, wait thou only upon God; for my expectation is from him...
Trust in him at all times; ye people, pour out your heart before him:
God is a refuge for us.

Psalm 62:5, 8

The best kind of waiting for the Christian is waiting upon God. In his time, our heavenly Father brings to pass our expectation. And what is expectation? It's faith that we will someday claim what God has promised. That's what promises are for. Unclaimed promises are as useless as nonexistent promises. To see the fruit of our expectation, we must walk in faith, waiting and trusting.

Pouring out one's heart before the Lord is cleansing—and it is practical. God hears our every lament. A poured-out heart is dear to our Creator's ear. For this reason, we can fully trust him at all times. He is and will always be our refuge.

Lord, many are the days in which I pour out my heart before you, knowing you hear. I lay before you my expectation in faith, claiming the promise of your provision. Father, I trust in you. You are my refuge, my hiding place.

Today's Takeaway

My expectation is from God alone.

I Thirst for You, O Lord

O God, thou art my God; early will I seek thee: my soul thirsteth for thee, my flesh longeth for thee in a dry and thirsty land, where no water is.

Psalm 63:1

We never think of hunger and thirst as positive desires—and yet it is our thirst for God that motivates us to move beyond "religion" in search of deeper fellowship with our true Father.

The psalmist wisely allowed his early morning thirst to drive him to seek God, to spy out that divine oasis in the dry and thirsty land of the desert.

Never think unkindly about your thirst for God. That yearning is a gift from the Lord, who is your rock and your defense. Trust him and never be moved.

Lord, thank you for my thirsty soul! Thank you for my flesh that longs for you. I can't imagine life without a yearning to know you more. Though I live in a world of deserts, I find living water in you when I seek you early. Fill me today, Father—to the brim and overflowing.

Today's Takeaway

My thirst for God is a good thirst. I will be satisfied.

I Lift Up My Hands in Thy Name

Because thy lovingkindness is better than life, my lips shall praise thee. Thus will I bless thee while I live: I will lift up my hands in thy name.

Psalm 63:3-4

The lifting of one's hands during worship can be seen as an act of surrender. And who better to surrender to than a God whose loving-kindness toward us is better than life itself?

Let's always allow our lips to praise him, to bless him. Let us freely lift our hands in his name. Let's have faith that our Creator will use our surrendered hands to help others. Let's believe God has plans to use our surrendered lives. Let's believe that with the Lord all things are possible.

God, there are few things better than life...but surely your loving-kindness is among them. Thus, my lips readily praise you. My hands are lifted to you in surrender. And not only my hands, but my entire self is yours.

O Lord, that your loving-kindness would shine through me so that others can see and receive your blessings!

—∞—

Today's Takeaway

I will bless God while I live.

Meditating on Thee in the Night Watches

My soul shall be satisfied as with marrow and fatness;
and my mouth shall praise thee with joyful lips:
When I remember thee upon my bed, and
meditate on thee in the night watches.

Psalm 63:5-6

Trouble sleeping? Try pondering the goodness of God, meditating on him as you recall his faithfulness during your day, looking ahead for a positive, Spirit-led tomorrow.

A satisfied soul always sleeps well. Let your worship of God lift you into restful slumber. May your final words as you fall asleep be praise with joyful lips.

Lord, I will praise you at all times. Early will I seek you. Then, in the night watches as I lay on my bed, my thoughts remain on you. I recall the events of the day now closing behind me. I consider your blessings and meditate on your goodness. I sleep well counting my blessings, looking for a bright tomorrow. When I awaken, I will again turn my thoughts to you.

—ɱ—

Today's Takeaway

I meditate on God as I drift off to sleep.

Hear My Prayer, O Lord

Hear my voice, O God, in my prayer: preserve my life from fear of the enemy.
Psalm 64:1

Each of us has many prayer needs. Some pray for restored health, others for healing of broken relationships. Some pray for this month's rent money, still others for relief from fear of an enemy. We may wonder if God really hears all these petitions. After all, we're each just one in eight billion people, many of whom have needs greater than our own.

The answer is yes. The Lord *does* hear our prayerful voices. Our greatest obstacle in prayer is believing he hears. It is also the easiest obstacle to overcome as we consider the greatness of the God to whom we are praying. How can we not believe he hears?

Pray on then!

Lord, forgive me when I doubt that you hear my prayers or when I don't have faith that you will answer. My problem is that I often walk by sight, not by faith. Though many voices cry out to you every day, you hear them all. There is no competition for your ear. You are the mighty God who hears.

Today's Takeaway

God hears my prayers and preserves my life.

God Crowns the Year with Goodness

Blessed is the man whom thou choosest, and causest to approach unto thee, that he may dwell in thy courts: we shall be satisfied with the goodness of thy house, even of thy holy temple... Thou crownest the year with thy goodness; and thy paths drop fatness.

Psalm 65:4, 11

Every Christian should be thankful for being chosen to receive the blessings of God when we exercise faith. We have earthly blessings here and eternal blessings in the house of the Lord.

Each year we pass on earth brings us just that much closer to our eternity with God. And yet, while we wait for the final year here, we can enjoy the fact that our Father is saying, "Not yet, beloved. Not yet." Though certainly God will show forth his goodness in greater detail in eternity, we can have a foretaste as we see him crown each additional year here with his goodness.

Yes, God is good, all the time. Eternity will reveal it. But don't wait until then. By faith today, accept that he is crowning your year with goodness.

Lord, you are my God who crowns my year with your goodness. You have chosen me to be a recipient of your blessings. For that, I rise up and bless you.

Today's Takeaway

This present life is just a foretaste of eternity with my God.

Tried as Silver

O bless our God, ye people, and make the voice of his praise to be heard: which holdeth our soul in life, and suffereth not our feet to be moved. For thou, O God, hast proved us: thou hast tried us, as silver is tried.

Psalm 66:8-10

Silver is tried through fire to remove the dross—the impurities. Likewise, when we are going through the fire of adversity, God removes the dross, proving us as his trusting children. We can either welcome trials as agents of God's grace or grumble about how unfair our adversities are.

Never fear the flames of the furnace. Welcome the purification. During the heat, make his praises known. He was in the furnace with Shadrach, Meshach, and Abednego. He will also be with you.

Lord, just as there was a fourth person with Shadrach, Meshach, and Abednego, so I know I am not not alone in the furnace. As I undergo whatever purification I need, please be with me. May I come out of the oven unscathed, all impurities removed.

Today's Takeaway

God uses the oven of life to remove my impurities.

My God Has Heard My Prayers

If I regard iniquity in my heart, the Lord will not hear me:
But verily God hath heard me; he hath attended to the voice of my prayer.
Blessed be God, which hath not turned away
my prayer, nor his mercy from me.
Psalm 66:18-20

It is a great loss when we regard iniquity in our heart. Relishing our sin causes a blockage between us and our Creator. God, who would welcome our prayers, is hindered by our rebellion. But sin confessed and forsaken demolishes the blockage, and the Lord attends to the voice of our prayers. He does not withhold mercy. Nor does he turn away our supplications—he welcomes them with open arms. Today, confess any known sin, receive by faith God's forgiveness, and walk away from all guilt.

Father, if there be any iniquity in me, please reveal it so I can repent and resume my effective prayer life. I know you are always ready to listen to my petitions, so turn me not away, nor withhold your mercy from me. Attend, O Lord, to my prayers.

Today's Takeaway

God attends to the voice of my prayers.

God, Our God, Shall Bless Us

Let the people praise thee, O God; let all the people praise thee.
Then shall the earth yield her increase; and God,
even our own God, shall bless us.
God shall bless us; and all the ends of the earth shall fear him.
Psalm 67:5-7

Consider that there is never a circumstance when praise is not appropriate. The psalmist beckons "all" the people to praise God. What happens then? We're told we reap the rewards of an earth yielding her increase and God blessing us. It's as simple as that: Praise releases the blessings of God. Note, too, that worship is very personal with God. Your neighbor cannot praise for you, nor can you praise for your neighbor.

If your earth is not yielding her increase, turn again and again to praise. A bountiful crop will be yours.

God, I desire your blessing above all else. Therefore, I will praise you—as I encourage others to join with me in worship. Thus will we enjoy your choicest blessings and delight in the fear of you. Lord, let our earth yield her increase.

Today's Takeaway

I praise God and receive his blessings.

Rejoice Exceedingly

Let the righteous be glad; let them rejoice before God: yea, let them exceedingly rejoice. Sing unto God, sing praises to his name: extol him that rideth upon the heavens by his name JAH, and rejoice before him.

Psalm 68:3-4

There is rejoicing, and then there is rejoicing *exceedingly*. When we worship, we're to be glad and rejoice and then we're to *re*-rejoice. Have we reached that level of rejoicing that can be described as "exceeding"? It's easy to do when we recall that the Lord's blessings for us are also exceeding. He gives, then gives again. Likewise, we rejoice and then we rejoice again. We extol him who rides upon the heavens by his name, *Jah*, which is the personal name of God in Hebrew.

Lord, today I choose to rejoice before you—not just rejoice, but re-rejoice! If I'm having a good day, rejoicing is expected and appropriate. If I'm having a bad day, there is even more reason to rejoice exceedingly. Extolling and singing your praises can change a bad day to a glad day.

Yes, Lord, I shall exult today. I shall praise your name, Jah*!*

Today's Takeaway

I rejoice in my God exceedingly!

A Family for Everyone

A father of the fatherless, and a judge of the widows, is God in his holy habitation. God setteth the solitary in families: he bringeth out those which are bound with chains: but the rebellious dwell in a dry land.
Psalm 68:5-6

God loves us all individually. But he also loves families. He *invented* families. In families we're able to see love for one another manifested. We're able to have acceptance from those nearest us. They rejoice with us, and they cry with us.

But what of those without a family? What about the fatherless? God cares for them. God loves to set the lonely, the solitary, and the fatherless in a family, whether it be a strong and supportive church family or literally a family that willingly opens their doors and offers that empty bedroom as a gift to Jesus. For when we provide a family for those without one, it is an offering to our Lord.

God, thank you for families. Thank you for providing for the fatherless, the widows, the solitary, and those bound with chains of addiction or other enslaving sins. Break their every chain, Lord. Set them in a family of your choosing.

Today's Takeaway

God created families as yet another of his blessings.

Daily Blessings from God

Blessed be the Lord, who daily loadeth us with benefits, even the God of our salvation. Selah. He that is our God is the God of salvation; and unto GOD *the Lord belong the issues from death.*

PSALM 68:19-20

How easily we forget our benefits as believers. Daily we enjoy blessing upon blessing that we take for granted. Let that not happen today. Watch closely for benefits you would normally miss. Make sure to include *unexpected* benefits. Count them and reflect on them at the day's end. And of all God's gifts, don't neglect to thank him for that priceless treasure that is your salvation. It is he who saves us from eternal death.

Lord, you have loaded me with benefits! I lack no good thing. You are the God who provides me with good gifts, including the most prized treasure of all, my salvation. You have marked out a day when I shall come to you through the death of this mortal body, which I will trade for an incorruptible body. I so long for that day, Father. Until then, I praise you for the many benefits you have given me.

—m—

Today's Takeaway

I receive daily benefits from the Lord.

My Sins Are Seen by God

O God, thou knowest my foolishness; and my sins are not hid from thee.
Psalm 69:5

We may be successful in concealing our sins and foolishness from others, but God sees us in *all* our folly and rebellion. For some that sounds like bad news. But in truth, it's good news. It was seeing our sin that caused God to make provision for our transgressions through the sacrifice of his Son. His full knowledge of our sins should make us all the more motivated to come to him, to confess the sins we're aware of and ask him to reveal any failings we have overlooked or excused ourselves from.

Father, you know me inside and out. You know my foolishness, and you know my limited wisdom. You even know my sins—they are laid bare before you. Thank you for the provision for my sins through the cross of Christ. Remind me, Lord, of failings I may have attempted to hide from even myself. May my life be an open book to you, Father.

Today's Takeaway

God's knowledge of our sins is good for us.

Set Me Up on High, Lord

I am poor and sorrowful: let thy salvation, O God, set me up on high.
Psalm 69:29

Blessed are those who know their true state. All things considered, we're all poor and sorrowful. That's why the words of "Amazing Grace" are so real to us. Without Christ, we are all, along with John Newton, "wretches." But it's in such a state that we're offered salvation. We are set free from our wretched status and set on high.

We are not paupers but are now sons and daughters of a king. What a blessed transaction is the cross that takes us from our low and lost standing to his high and holy standing.

God, it is truly amazing grace that sets me up on high. In reality, I belong among the lowly. I have nothing to boast about, save my faith in Christ—and even that is a gift. Here, then, is one more "wretch" whom you have lifted on high.

Today's Takeaway

I'm a child of the King, set on high with the Lord.

Make Haste, Lord

Let all those that seek thee rejoice and be glad in thee: and let such as love thy salvation say continually, Let God be magnified. But I am poor and needy: make haste unto me, O God: thou art my help and my deliverer; O Lord, make no tarrying.

Psalm 70:4-5

We have prayed for God to speed his answer to our prayers. We wish he would indeed "make haste" to deliver us. But what is faith if not the willingness to let the Lord set the times for our deliverance? It's not wrong to pray for God to answer our prayers quickly, but it is wrong to fault him for being late in answering.

So when you pray, don't give God a deadline by which he must answer. Trust him not only with the answer but also with the timing.

God, may you be magnified! Glory to your name! I have prayed for many things, Lord, and so many of my petitions have been answered. Others still await your answer…in your time. And yet, I must ask you again: Make haste unto me, O Father, my helper and deliverer. Make no tarrying!

Today's Takeaway

May God be magnified in my life.

More Praise

Let them be confounded and consumed that are adversaries to my soul;
let them be covered with reproach and dishonor that seek my hurt.
But I will hope continually, and will yet praise thee more and more.

Psalm 71:13-14

Hoping continually is never giving up despite the many adversaries to our souls.

Praising more and more is also never giving up, as is being thankful. And so is our willingness to wait on God for the answer.

Is there something for which you are tempted to give up on praying? A relationship? A lost son or daughter? A financial burden? A troubling medical diagnosis? A ministry? A dream?

Any and all of these are in God's care and must be left there. We can ask. We can hope. We can praise. All three must be done continually until we have an answer. And when God says wait, then wait we must.

O Lord, despite my adversaries, despite my troubling circumstances, I will hope continually. I will ask continually. I will praise you continually. And I will wait.

The answer is on the way.

—ʊʊ—

Today's Takeaway

I will hope continually in the Lord.

Not My Strength, But His

I will go in the strength of the Lord God: I will make mention of thy righteousness, even of thine only. O God, thou hast taught me from my youth: and hitherto have I declared thy wondrous works. Now also when I am old and grayheaded, O God, forsake me not; until I have showed thy strength unto this generation, and thy power to every one that is to come.

Psalm 71:16-18

When we go in our own strength, we're likely to fail. Why? Because our strength has its limits. But when we set aside our strength and go in *God's* strength, we're going in unlimited strength. Consider that there is no force, no circumstance, no enemy for which God cannot be our strength. Make it your practice to always "go in the strength of the Lord God." Seasoned believers, with their gray heads, have seen God move on their behalf. If you are not yet gray, you will be one day. You will look back and remember our Creator's faithfulness.

Lord, truth be told, I have no strength for the challenges I face. You have been my God for lo these many years. You have been my right arm in battle. Today, as with yesterday, I go in the strength of you, my Lord God.

Today's Takeaway

I will go in the strength of the Lord God.

We Are Blessed in Him

His name shall endure for ever: his name shall
be continued as long as the sun:
and men shall be blessed in him: all nations shall call him blessed. Blessed
be the Lord *God, the God of Israel, who only doeth wondrous things.*
And blessed be his glorious name for ever: and let the whole
earth be filled with his glory; amen, and amen.
Psalm 72:17-19

Think of it. The source of all blessings is our God, whose name shall endure forever. One day all nations shall call him blessed. His glorious name will ring throughout eternity. And yet here, in this time and this place, we are privileged to know him and be blessed in him. He is the Lord who only does wondrous things. Just look around. Remember his past victories in your life.

Call him blessed today and every day.

Lord, your name shall endure forever. You exist beyond all time. You are Lord of all creation, and someday all nations shall call you blessed. Today I call you blessed.

Today's Takeaway

My God is the source of all blessing.

My Solitary Desire, O Lord

Thou shalt guide me with thy counsel, and afterward receive me to glory.
Whom have I in heaven but thee? and there is
none upon earth that I desire beside thee.
My flesh and my heart faileth: but God is the strength
of my heart, and my portion for ever.
Psalm 73:24-26

Truly, is there anything we could desire in this life that is better than knowing our Lord? Is there anything to be enjoyed in heaven other than our God? Is there any better counsel we can receive than that which our Creator offers?

What, after all, will make heaven *heaven*? Surely, it's the very presence of our Lord. The richest blessing for the believer is desiring God both now and in eternity.

Your flesh will fail someday. So will your heart. But if God is your portion, he will never fail you. Not now and not in eternity.

God, others have failed me, and I have failed myself. But you have never failed me, even though I often didn't understand your plan. Lord, take my insufficient heart and my humble flesh. You are my portion and my wise counselor.

Today's Takeaway

There is none on earth I desire beside God.

THE GOD OF ALL CREATION

The day is thine, the night also is thine: thou hast prepared the light and the sun. Thou hast set all the borders of the earth: thou hast made summer and winter.

PSALM 74:16-17

God has set natural boundaries on planet earth. Night and day. Sun and darkness. The borders of the earth, the seasons, and much more.

Apart from nature, he has also set boundaries for us—often behavioral limits. We know most of the boundaries through Scripture. We know not to steal, murder, lie, covet, cheat, and more.

Some boundaries may be unique to us and known only to us. A person who has troubles with certain internet sites may need to install a filter as a barrier to sites he or she must not visit. A person with a weakness for gambling must avoid casinos. A person given to gluttony must set boundaries with their appetites.

Do you know and respect your limits?

Lord, I love the natural boundaries you have placed in this world. I also appreciate that you have given me guidelines and limits in order for me to have a happy and productive life. When new boundaries must be set in place due to my weakness, please help me know each new limit quickly so I can avoid the heartache caused by violating safe boundaries.

Today's Takeaway

God has designed both natural boundaries and spiritual boundaries.

Thanks Be to God

Unto thee, O God, do we give thanks, unto thee do we give thanks: for that thy name is near thy wondrous works declare.

Psalm 75:1

Isn't it interesting that the psalmist tells us God's wondrous works declare the *nearness* of our Creator, through the nearness of his name? As is common with so many other elements in the Psalms, the result when we ponder this is that we are prompted to give thanks.

Do you, perhaps, need a reminder that God is near to you today? Do you need the assurance of his presence?

If so, just look around. His wondrous works are speaking to you. Their message is stronger than words can say...but we still may hear the good news of his presence.

Lord, I hear you speak to me through your wondrous works and your Word. Your nearness declares your glorious name. So, unto you, Father, thanks is due. Your works resound with your presence.

Today's Takeaway

I thank God for all his wondrous works.

Promotion Comes from God

For promotion cometh neither from the east, nor
from the west, nor from the south.
But God is the judge: he putteth down one, and setteth up another.
Psalm 75:6-7

When we think it's time for us to be noted and promoted, set up higher than we are, it's hard to wait. We want to push things along. We want to be noticed. We want to be promoted, to be told, "Come up higher." But that's not God's way. *He* is the promoter.

Place your cause before him. Let him have the controls. You do *not* want a promotion that is not from the Lord.

O God, I praise you for your sovereignty over all your creation. You raise up and you bring down. There are times when I want to be noticed, promoted, even honored for my accomplishments. But such a human want is beneath me. I must leave all promotion and all notice up to you—and remember that, even when I am honored, it is you being honored since you alone raise me up and put me down. I can take no credit for that which originates in you.

Today's Takeaway

Promotion comes from God.

God's One Desire

Vow, and pay unto the Lord your God: let all that be round about him bring presents unto him that ought to be feared.

Psalm 76:11

What can one pay to the Lord? He needs no money, no gold, no real estate. These already belong to God and are of no worth to him. The one thing he desires above all else is the gift of our surrendered life.

Why should we, the created, withhold from him, the Creator, that to which he has a right? If we truly fear him as Lord, we will gladly gift him with ourselves.

It's really all we have to give.

Lord, what do I have to offer you, my creator and redeemer? You have no need of material things. There is nothing on this planet that you do not already own. As for me, I have nothing but myself to give—and amazingly, that's the one gift you want.

So, Father, today I again commit my way to you. Bring into my life the circumstances and people of your choosing. Let there be opportunities to trust you more fully.

Today's Takeaway

My life is all I have to offer God...and that's all he wants.

Calling to Remembrance Thy Wonders of Old

I will remember the works of the LORD: surely
I will remember thy wonders of old.
I will meditate also of all thy work, and talk of thy doings.
PSALM 77:11-12

Memory is a blessed gift of God. Painful memories linger but can be replaced by considering the past works of the Lord—even his "wonders of old" both in our life and in his creation.

Pondering the works of God brings us a fresh sense of awe and a renewed trust in our heavenly Father.

Best of all, meditating on God's works will soon cause us to talk of his mighty doings. His past goodness to us should assure us of our future blessings at his hand.

O Lord, what a pleasure it is to recall the ways you've come through for me in the past. When I've needed you, you have always been near. Such memories refresh my hopes for the future. You will never change. Your faithfulness is not just a past faithfulness, but a present and future faithfulness as well. Yes, Father, I meditate on your work and talk of your doings.

Today's Takeaway

I will meditate on God's past goodness to me and his wonders of old.

For the Generation to Come

Give ear, O my people, to my law: incline your ears to the words of my mouth.
I will open my mouth in a parable: I will utter dark sayings of old: which we have heard and known, and our fathers have told us.
We will not hide them from their children, showing to the generation to come the praises of the LORD, and his strength, and his wonderful works that he hath done.

PSALM 78:1-4

Once again we're called upon to contemplate the wonderful works of God—but now with the exhortation to pass along to our children the very same things our fathers taught us. We must never hide the goodness of God from our children, nor neglect to show them his strength. It will serve them well and, if we've done our job faithfully, our children will pass along the testimony to the next generation.

Father, you are the Lord of all generations. Hundreds of past generations could testify to your goodness if they could speak from the grave. While I yet live, I will praise you daily and commit to passing along the knowledge of your faithfulness to the generations after me.

It's a great thing to know that there never has been nor ever will be a generation without the knowledge of you.

Today's Takeaway

The presence of the Lord will abide throughout all generations.

Thy Tender Mercies

O remember not against us former iniquities:
let thy tender mercies speedily prevent us: for we are brought very low. Help us, O God of our salvation, for the glory of thy name: and deliver us, and purge away our sins, for thy name's sake.

Psalm 79:8-9

What would our life be like if the Creator remembered our iniquities and charged us with the guilt due us? What a dismal thought. But, praise God, we can pray for his forgetfulness of our sins, no matter how many—no matter how awful—and experience his forgiveness. They have all been purged.

Our every sin has been dealt with in the only way possible—through the cross of Christ. Oh yes, God's tender mercies never fail, no matter how low we have fallen.

Lord, should my sins remain, I would be lost...brought very low indeed. But with the psalmist I can pray that you no longer remember my former iniquities. Your tender mercies are ever present, ever forgiving, ever offering grace. Thank you, Father, for your divine forgetfulness. May I, too, forget my many past sins.

Today's Takeaway

God has dealt fully with all my sins. I am thankful!

Cause Thy Glorious Face to Shine

Turn us again, O God, and cause thy face
to shine; and we shall be saved.
Psalm 80:3

The pattern was repeated over and over. The Israelites called out to God, and he saved them and prospered them. Then sin entered in, and God seemingly withdrew, resulting in misery. So once again, the people prayed, "Turn us again, O God, and cause thy face to shine; and we shall be saved."

It is a grievous consideration to think of God's face being turned away from us—and thank God it never is, though at times it may feel to be so.

On the other hand, it's a glorious thought to know that God's face always shines upon us. It is amazing that his grace continually saves us.

If there's any turning to be done, it is we who must turn away from ourselves and face our Lord, whose face shines upon us with love.

Lord, do not turn your face from me. Let the radiance of your love shine on me today. Keep me from turning inward to self; help me turn toward your face of love.

Today's Takeaway

God's face is ever toward me.

The God Who Feeds Us

I am the LORD thy God, which brought thee out of the land of Egypt: open thy mouth wide, and I will fill it.

Psalm 81:10

If we are hungry or unfed, it is not the fault of God. We have only to open our mouths wide and he promises to fill them. After all, he is the God who supplied the Israelites with fresh manna every morning as they trekked away from Egypt.

They were supplied by the Lord—and so are we. He is the God who multiplied the loaves and the fishes to feed a multitude. He has not changed.

Open wide your mouth today. He will fill it.

O God, you know my hunger—not for my daily bread but for you. I well remember how you brought me out of spiritual Egypt, just as you brought your people out of geographical Egypt. You fed them daily and you feed me with yourself daily.

Just as I open my mouth wide to be fed, you supply the true Bread of Life that nourishes me, fills me, and contents me.

Today's Takeaway

If I will open my mouth to receive, God will provide.

Defend and Deliver

God standeth in the congregation of the
mighty; he judgeth among the gods.
How long will ye judge unjustly, and accept
the persons of the wicked? Selah.
Defend the poor and fatherless: do justice to the afflicted and needy.
Deliver the poor and needy: rid them out of the hand of the wicked.

Psalm 82:1-4

God calls us to many things—including judging justly, refusing the wicked person, defending the poor and fatherless, bringing forth justice for the afflicted and needy, and delivering the poor and needy out of the hand of the wicked one.

How are we to do this? God will gladly show each of us our part to play in obeying this divine directive. We have only to ask, listen, and *do*. The result of our doing—whether it be praying, supporting financially, or rolling up our sleeves and getting our hands dirty—will be blessing for those we minister to. To neglect those in need is to neglect Christ himself.

God, you have given me a role to play in attending to the poor and fatherless, the afflicted and needy. You call me to help deliver the captives from the hand of the wicked. Show me daily how I can help those in need.

Today's Takeaway

If I neglect the poor and needy, I neglect Christ.

Lord, Be Not Still

Keep not thou silence, O God: hold not thy peace, and be not still, O God. For, lo, thine enemies make a tumult: and they that hate thee have lifted up the head.

Psalm 83:1-2

We become impatient if God doesn't speak. When reading his Word is dry, when our prayers don't go beyond the ceiling, when our church fellowship is boring and the sermons summon sleep, we are most keenly aware of our Creator's silence.

But is he really silent? Surely God is always awake, always listening to our prayers, and, yes, speaking. It then is clear that it is *we* who cannot hear, not God who is silent. Asking the Lord to be not still is valid, but it's useless to pray so if we don't also ask for ears to hear and a willingness to act.

God, once again, like David, I ask that I hear your voice, that you not be seemingly silent. The enemies of truth abound. They rise in accusation against you. They attack me with temptations to doubt. O Lord, quiet the tumult of the enemies. Silence their voices, not your own.

Be not still, O God!

Today's Takeaway

In God's seeming silence, he is yet present.

My Soul Longs for God

My soul longeth, yea, even fainteth for the courts of the Lord: my heart and my flesh crieth out for the living God.

Psalm 84:2

The true test of our faith is to discern what causes us to hunger. Is our appetite for money? Fame? Personal achievement? Accomplishing any or all of those is worthless when we slip into eternity.

Lovers of God can live and die without these achievements, but what we cannot live without is a deep heart hunger to know more of God. It's a desire the Lord both implants in us and fulfills as we feast on him through prayer and his Word.

Longing, fainting, crying out for the living God—that's our true test of faith.

Lord, longing for you is surely a gift you implant in our hearts. On our own, we would not seek you—and in fact, many do not seek you. This longing I feel is a godly hunger that will not be denied. My heart cries out for you, O God. Satisfy with the knowledge of your presence.

Today's Takeaway

When I cry out to the living God, he answers every time.

The House of My God

For a day in thy courts is better than a thousand.
I had rather be a doorkeeper in the house of my God,
than to dwell in the tents of wickedness.
Psalm 84:10

What awaits those who prefer to dwell in the tents of wickedness rather than be a servant in the house of God? There is a stark contrast between the two. The former will live in sheer godless darkness forever. The latter, through God's grace, will dwell with their loving Father in a full spectrum of light.

Being a doorkeeper for God is a highly exalted position and one we can all easily aspire to.

Lord, I shudder when I think of the fate of those who dwell in the tents of wickedness. Darkness abounds. Your presence is not known. O God, how far better to be even a lowly doorkeeper in your house than to abide with the wicked. Yet I suspect in your house there are no lowly positions.

Yes, to be with you for one day is far better than a thousand elsewhere. Grant it, O Lord.

Today's Takeaway

I will gladly take a lowly position if it so pleases God.

The God of Grace and Glory

For the Lord God is a sun and shield: the Lord will give grace and glory: no good thing will he withhold from them that walk uprightly. O Lord of hosts, blessed is the man that trusteth in thee.

Psalm 84:11-12

God is forever a giver. Of his many gifts, grace and glory are high on the list. Our Creator is so giving that he withholds no good thing from his people—those who walk uprightly. Further, he is a sun and a shield to us, giving protection, warmth, and light.

We are blessed because we trust in him.

Father, when I want a blessing, I must trust in you for it—and then wait prayerfully. Your blessings do come, but they come in your time, not mine. As I pray and wait, I will remind myself that you withhold no good thing from me and that your grace and glory are gifts for me. If I were the only person on the planet, you would still attend to my needs. If I have you, what really do I lack?

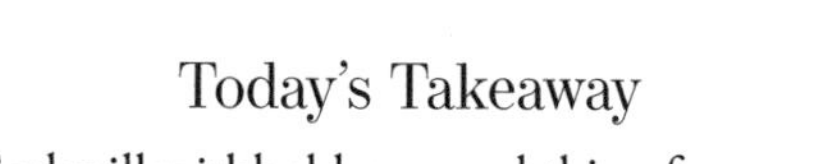

Today's Takeaway

God will withhold no good thing from me.

A Divine Meeting of Mercy and Truth

Mercy and truth are met together; righteousness
and peace have kissed each other.
Truth shall spring out of the earth; and righteousness
shall look down from heaven.
Yea, the LORD shall give that which is good;
and our land shall yield her increase.
Righteousness shall go before him; and shall set us in the way of his steps.

PSALM 85:10-13

One would be hard-pressed to enumerate the virtues of God. Mercy and truth are mentioned here, and his righteousness and his peace are depicted as loving companions. Truth and righteousness are ever present. God is a giver of that which is good and blesses our "land" with a fruitful yield.

We should take care to never allow disparaging thoughts of our Creator to dwell in our minds. All such venomous considerations are designed to denigrate the Lord's character. Have none of it.

Father, you are the God of all virtues. There is no positive character quality that you lack. When we grow in you, these qualities take root in our lives, and we become more like you as we are set in the way of your steps. We shall be blessed as our land yields a good crop.

Today's Takeaway

The Lord gives that which is good.

Walking in Truth

Teach me thy way, O Lord; I will walk in thy
truth: unite my heart to fear thy name.
I will praise thee, O Lord my God, with all my heart:
and I will glorify thy name for evermore.
Psalm 86:11-12

With God as our teacher, we become wise, enabled to walk in the truth he's taught us. Walking in truth means to take our steps forward based on the truth of God's Word.

Our other option—chosen by many—is to walk in our own ways, not according to truth.

We know where that leads. Don't go there!

We all are given the raw material for life. Some would say it's easier to succeed for those born into prosperity. But while that may be true here in this life, it offers no eternal advantage. And eternity is where our life is rooted.

Lord, be my teacher. Lead me to walk in your truth. Remind me to always walk in the righteous fear of you. As I gain the wisdom you teach me, I will glorify your name forevermore.

Today's Takeaway

God teaches me his ways, but I must listen.

Springs in the Desert

All my springs are in thee.
Psalm 87:7

We are sometimes dry and thirsty in search of cool water. What this world offers as "springs" are mere mirages in the desert. If we pursue them in search of refreshment, we find the dry dust of disappointment. We end up spitting out sand.

God, however, offers not a mirage but an oasis, bringing true refreshment: cool waters to sustain us through this trek across the desert. In him we find all our needful springs. But to get to the oasis, we must be willing to bypass the alluring mirages of this sandy world.

God, you have seen my past days of trying to partake of earthly springs. But they never satisfied. The wisest thing I ever did was leave the desert behind and head for the true springs of joy I find in you. I have washed the gritty taste of sand from my mouth.

Now I find all my springs in you.

Today's Takeaway

No earthly springs can satisfy like God's springs of living water.

I Stretch Out My Hands to Thee

O Lord God of my salvation, I have cried day and night before thee:
Let my prayer come before thee: incline thine ear unto my cry;
for my soul is full of troubles: and my life draweth nigh unto the grave...
Mine eye mourneth by reason of affliction:
Lord, I have called daily upon thee,
I have stretched out my hands unto thee.

Psalm 88:1-3, 9

David knew what to do when afflicted: He called *daily* on God, stretching out his hands toward heaven. His affliction was great, but he knew his Redeemer was the great healer of affliction. If you are currently afflicted, follow David. Call on the Lord. Cry out to God. Stretch out your hands. He will comfort your mourning eyes.

O God, I am in a season of trial and trouble. In past times of woe, you have seen me through. I now ask you to walk through this present adversity with me. Daily do I call on you with outstretched hands. Dry the tears from these mourning eyes. Comfort my afflicted soul. Incline your ear to my cries. Be present with me in this time of need.

Today's Takeaway

There is no trouble in my life for which God does not have a solution.

The Joyful Sound

Blessed is the people that know the joyful sound:
they shall walk, O Lord, in the light of thy countenance.
Psalm 89:15

Not everyone hears the joyful sound. Only those who listen for it will hear the songs of heaven. Those who *do* hear find that they're enabled to walk confidently in the light of his countenance.

Though troubles nip at our soul and our life draws near to the grave, we will trust in God and walk in his countenance.

O Lord, I hear the joyful sound. It moves me to walk in the light of your countenance. Even during the hardest of times, I hear the often-faint melody that beckons me on. And the closer I get to the end of my troubles, the louder the joyful sound.

Father, incline your ear unto my cry. Hear me recount my trials and sorrows.

Cue the joyful sound.

Today's Takeaway

I am blessed to be among those who hear the joyful sound.

From Everlasting to Everlasting

Lord, thou hast been our dwelling place in all generations. Before the mountains were brought forth, or ever thou hadst formed the earth and the world, even from everlasting to everlasting, thou art God.

Psalm 90:1-2

It's good to ponder the agelessness of God. He is Lord from everlasting in the past until everlasting in the future. He knows no limits in time. He even invented the concept of time.

He who formed this world keeps watch over all his people—from generation to generation.

There is comfort in contemplating the vastness and the timelessness of the Creator. To think that he, the Almighty One, considers frail mankind with tender care—the contrast is astonishing.

Father, you existed before time began. You will exist when time is no longer. And yet you have created puny men and women to be objects of your love. You have even granted us the gift of eternal life. As regards our future, we too are ageless!

O God, in all things, you are Lord.

Today's Takeaway

My God is ageless, from eternity past to eternity future.

Our Timeless God

For a thousand years in thy sight are but as yesterday when it is past, and as a watch in the night.

Psalm 90:4

God is not dependent on time. We, however, are. The Lord knows and controls the future before we see it unfold. Events, good and bad, surprise us; but God knew all along. Not only does our Creator see events coming our way, but he also acts to incorporate those events into his perfect will for those who will walk by faith, trusting him.

We need not fear the passage of time. The Lord has seen our future, and we are secure. He considers yesterday as no different than a thousand years.

As in Psalm 89, the psalmist here confirms the timeless nature of God. When we see our lives as a brief speck on the timeline of the Lord's creation, we can realize the ultimate smallness of our problems. Our timeless God sees the future—and when we trust in what he sees, we can rest in his wisdom.

God, you are the inventor of time. Time is the tool you use to unfold history. You are the keeper of my time. As I number my days, help me to both enjoy you more and serve you more effectively. Thank you for every minute of time you are allowing me here on earth. May I make the most of each moment.

Today's Takeaway

Time is never a consideration with God. He is never late, never early.

Numbering Our Days

So teach us to number our days, that we may apply our hearts unto wisdom.
Psalm 90:12

Many of us see our days drift by without any obvious purpose. Days turn into weeks, weeks into years, and we soon are gone. But in all those years, did we number our days—that is, did we make them count? Or did they all passively fly by until the inevitable arrival of our final day?

It's not too late for us to take more seriously our time on earth so we can apply our hearts to wisdom and value our days. God holds the key. He's the one to teach us to number our days...but he can't do it if we are careless with time. Each day, week, month, and year is a gift to us. God asks us how we will use them. What will we answer? Let it be the psalmist's plea: Lord, "teach us to number our days."

Lord, my days are numbered. Though I don't know that final number, you do. So teach me how to make the most of my remaining days. Let wisdom, not emotion, rule my heart in the time I have left.

Today's Takeaway

God teaches me to be mindful of my limited number of days on earth.

The Secret Place

He that dwelleth in the secret place of the most High
shall abide under the shadow of the Almighty.
Psalm 91:1

All of us want to dwell in safety. But where do we find the ultimate in safety? Surely it's by dwelling in the secret place of the Most High. The *secret* place. A place where trouble, sorrow, and danger can't find us.

Here in this hidden place we abide under the mighty shadow of the Almighty. We must each, by faith, make the secret place our dwelling. God is willing to receive us. We must be willing to make our abode under his mighty shadow.

Lord, when trouble comes my way, you are my secret place. I run to you and seek shelter under your almighty shadow. Even when all is well and trouble is absent, I come to dwell in my secret place. For not only is it a shelter for me, but it is also a meeting place where I enjoy fellowship with you. Hide me, Father, under your protective shadow. Meet me there.

Today's Takeaway

There is no safer place for me than under the shadow of the Almighty.

No Fear

Thou shalt not be afraid for the terror by night;
nor for the arrow that flieth by day;
nor for the pestilence that walketh in darkness;
nor for the destruction that wasteth at noonday.
A thousand shall fall at thy side, and ten thousand at
thy right hand; but it shall not come nigh thee.
Psalm 91:5-7

What are your fears? Do you have a fear that God is unable to release you from? It's impossible to say yes to that question. God intervenes when fear arises, no matter the cause. It may be night terror, day terror, pestilence, destruction, or any number of natural or man-made threats. Others may fall by the thousands, but God's promise is that it "shall not come nigh thee."

Father, you have taken away my fears. I no longer need to worry or be anxious, for you have already seen how my future unfolds—it will be good, and it will be fearless. No terror shall grip me, nor shall I fear disease or pestilence. Though a thousand shall fall at my side, I can be safe from destruction. Thus is my heritage as your child.

Today's Takeaway

I fear nothing. God is my protector from all that would destroy me.

No Evil Shall Befall Me

Because thou hast made the LORD, which is my refuge, even the most High, thy habitation; there shall no evil befall thee, neither shall any plague come nigh thy dwelling. For he shall give his angels charge over thee, to keep thee in all thy ways.

PSALM 91:9-11

How are we kept safe during evil threats? We're sheltered by his angels, who have been charged by God to watch over us and to keep us *in all our ways*. No evil shall conquer us. No plague shall claim us. No temptation shall overcome us. God is our refuge and habitation!

Lord, evil is rampant today. It's easy to be fearful just watching the evening news. But the antidote to fearing evil is to fear you and run to you as my habitation from evil. Even dangerous plagues are not a cause for fear when I know that you've put angels in charge over me. Surely they shall keep me from fearing evil.

Today's Takeaway

The Lord is my safe habitation.

The Flourishing Christian

The righteous shall flourish like the palm tree:
he shall grow like a cedar in Lebanon.
Those that be planted in the house of the Lord
shall flourish in the courts of our God.
They shall still bring forth fruit in old age;
they shall be fat and flourishing;
to show that the Lord *is upright: he is my rock,*
and there is no unrighteousness in him.

Psalm 92:12-15

God wants his people to not just exist but *flourish*. We are to be healthy plants in the house of the Lord—even through our old age. Why? To show that the Creator is upright. Always and forever righteous, he is our rock and will be forever.

Lord, I am righteous because of Christ. He is my righteousness. Your promise is that I shall flourish like a palm tree and grow like a cedar in Lebanon. You have planted me, and you will water and feed me through a fruitful old age. Thus shall you be known as upright. You are my rock, my heavenly gardener, my righteousness.

Today's Takeaway

My life shall flourish, even in old age.

Higher Ground

The floods have lifted up, O Lord, the floods have lifted up their voice; the floods lift up their waves. The Lord on high is mightier than the noise of many waters, yea, than the mighty waves of the sea.

Psalm 93:3-4

What do we do during a flood? If we're wise, we move to higher ground—and higher ground is where the Lord abides. He is mightier than the floods that threaten us. He rolls back the tidal waves of the sea that pour into our lives. His love washes over us as a cleansing tide.

If today finds you at sea with troubles, move by faith to the higher ground. Move to where the Lord on high abides.

Mighty is our God!

Lord, today I declare your might. You have lifted me higher than the floodwaters that would consume me. Your voice is more powerful than the noise of the thrashing waves. While the enemy brings a rushing torrent of trouble, you bring a tsunami of love for your children. Praise your name, Father!

Today's Takeaway

The Lord is my higher ground when floods threaten.

God Will Never Forsake His Dear Children

The LORD will not cast off his people, neither will he forsake his inheritance… In the multitude of my thoughts within me thy comforts delight my soul.

Psalm 94:14, 19

Some people often wonder if there's anything God cannot do. The answer is yes. God cannot cast off his people. He cannot forsake his inheritance. We who are his are his forever. He has purchased us and that without "buyer's remorse." Stay firm in the knowledge that the one thing your heavenly Father cannot do is abandon you. Delight your soul in thoughts of his comfort. Rest secure in his faithfulness.

Lord, thank you for the security of knowing I'm yours forever. You will never forsake me nor cast me off. My thoughts are constantly on your greatness and your many comforts that delight my soul. Your thoughts are toward me, always. You are the God of the forsaken, who will never forsake his own.

Today's Takeaway

God will never forsake me. Neither will I turn away from him.

Kneeling Before Our God

O come, let us worship and bow down: let us kneel before the Lord our maker.
For he is our God; and we are the people of his pasture, and the sheep of his hand.
Psalm 95:6-7

God hears all our prayers: those we say while standing, sitting, prostrate, and kneeling. But there is power in our knees. Think of all we can do just because we have knees. We stand with our knees. We walk and run enabled by our knees. And when we kneel before the Lord, it's a way of submitting to our Creator. It's a way of honoring him. We can't kneel every time we pray, but we can kneel sometimes as we pray. In our every prayer we can give the Lord the glory and strength due his name.

Father, today I worship you in the beauty of holiness. I pray to you on bended knees. I pray to you standing, sitting, and even prostrate. No matter my stance, my heart is always bowed before you as I give you the glory due your name.

May all the earth fear you in love.

Today's Takeaway

I can pray effectively kneeling, standing, walking, or even prostrate.

The Lord, Our God, Is Great

For the Lord is great, and greatly to be praised:
he is to be feared above all gods.
For all the gods of the nations are idols: but the Lord made the heavens.
Psalm 96:4-5

After all these centuries of mankind on earth, we still witness idol worship. And it's not just among faraway primitive people that we find idolatry. Modern man has his idols of money, fame, personal glory. And yes, some still bow down to images or idols made by human hands.

To be sure, people *will* find something to worship. But there is only one God, and he alone is worthy of our worship. To adore and reverence an idol—any idol—is to rob God of the glory due him.

Demolish any idols you have and stay clear from the attraction of future idols.

God, I don't understand why some people choose to worship idols that can do nothing for them. You are the true God, and you alone are worthy of the worship some unbelievers give to their idols. Lord, for those caught up in idolatry, I pray you would open their eyes to see their folly. Open their eyes to worship you alone.

Today's Takeaway

I reject the worship of all idols, past or present.
My God is the only living God!

Saved from the Hand of the Wicked

Ye that love the Lord, hate evil: he preserveth the souls of his saints; he delivereth them out of the hand of the wicked.

Psalm 97:10

Evil in its many forms has always plagued man, starting in the Garden of Eden. It still exists today—not passively but actively. It wears many disguises as it searches for new victims. Don't let yourself become a casualty to evil.

Our response to wickedness must always be to hate it vehemently, to turn away from it. And—heaven forbid—should we fall into its clutches, we must cry out to God to be delivered and then by faith walk away from every hint of iniquity.

Do not try to compromise. To compromise with evil is to lose the battle.

Lord, the enemy of our souls has tried since the Garden of Eden to seduce us through lies and deception. I pray you will open my eyes to his tactics when I see him trying to deceive me or pull me into sin. Father, be quick to save me from the hand of the wicked. Keep me alive to righteousness and dead to evil.

Today's Takeaway

God delivers me from the hand of the wicked.

A Joyful Noise

Make a joyful noise unto the Lord, all the earth: make a loud noise, and rejoice, and sing praise.
Sing unto the Lord with the harp; with the harp, and the voice of a psalm.
With trumpets and sound of cornet make a joyful noise before the Lord, the King.

Psalm 98:4-6

The "noise" God loves is the joyful praise that leaves no doubt as to the object of the praise. The God who often speaks through silence also hears loud rejoicing. Not just our voices, but also the joyful noises of harps, trumpets, and cornets.

It's likely that praise from any instrument or voice is welcome in heaven. Don't only whisper your praises; make an occasional *loud* joyful noise. God will hear—and so will heaven.

Father, I praise you in silence, and I praise you in a loud voice, making a joyful noise. You have made all things work together for good for me, and the result is a heart full of joy. It's a gladness that cannot be taken from me. It's eternal *joy.*

Hear, O Lord, my joy-filled praises, both silent and loud. All glory to you!

Today's Takeaway

God loves it when I make a joyful noise as I worship him.

EXALT OUR HOLY GOD

Exalt ye the LORD our God, and worship at his footstool; for he is holy…
Exalt the LORD our God, and worship at his
holy hill; for the LORD our God is holy.
PSALM 99:5, 9

Our human nature causes us to search for opportunities to exalt self. Such personal puffery pleases us on one level. Self-adulation is based, however, on the false premise that we are worthy due to our own efforts. But we know better. Quite the opposite is true. We are blessed because of him, not because of us. Exaltation belongs to the Lord…for *he* alone is holy.

Exalt the Lord today. Give him the fresh praises that are due him. Doing so will increase your joy, no matter what the day holds.

Lord God, today I exalt you. I worship at your footstool, for you are holy. You are worthy of all praise and honor. With my whole heart, I magnify you. I raise the banners of praise in your name. Yes, be exalted, O God! I rejoice mightily in you!

Today's Takeaway

God is to be exalted!

We Are the Sheep of His Pasture

Make a joyful noise unto the Lord, all ye lands.
Serve the Lord with gladness: come before his presence with singing.
Know ye that the Lord he is God: it is he that hath made us, and not we ourselves; we are his people, and the sheep of his pasture.
Enter into his gates with thanksgiving, and into his courts with praise: be thankful unto him, and bless his name.
For the Lord is good; his mercy is everlasting; and his truth endureth to all generations.

Psalm 100

May it never be that we meet a "self-made Christian." Even if it were possible, such a creature would be grotesque. God alone is the maker of Christians.

It is through the new birth of the Holy Spirit that we become a sheep in his pasture. We would scoff at the idea of a proud, self-made sheep and just as ludicrous is the self-made Christian. Know that he is God and that he has made us.

Lord, I'm just another sheep in your pasture. Yet I know if I were lost, you would leave the ninety-nine and come looking for me. Why? Because you have made me; I have not made myself. Your goodness and mercy are everlasting, and your truth endures for all generations.

Today's Takeaway

Contentment comes from grazing in the Father's pasture.

Behaving Wisely

I will behave myself wisely in a perfect way.
O when wilt thou come unto me?
I will walk within my house with a perfect heart.
Psalm 101:2

How can we have a perfect heart? How can we behave in a perfect way? The answer, as always, is by faith. We have been saved from our old selves and are now living by faith in the Son of God.

So now we abide in the power of the "new creation," and our hearts do not condemn us. To have no guilt is walking with a perfect heart. To be cleansed from sin by faith in the blood of Christ is to walk wisely in a perfect way. Is it not the greatest of news that our sins have been forgiven and the righteousness of Christ has been imputed to us?

Oh yes, this is great news indeed!

Father, left to my own devices, I will surely fail. Teach me, then, to behave wisely in a perfect way. Lead me in the ways of those whose hearts are perfect. Instruct me in the ways of the new creation. Thank you for my imputed righteousness.

May I walk in faith, not by sight, trusting in you.

Today's Takeaway

I walk in a perfect way by faith.

Guarding My Eyes

I will set no wicked thing before mine eyes.
Psalm 101:3

Sinful attractions seem to be everywhere: TV, movies, books, music. We live in a culture sympathetic to immorality and wickedness. It's up to us to "set no wicked thing" before our eyes. The TV has a remote. No one is dragging us to impure movies. We are not compelled to visit websites that portray sexual immorality or flirtations with the occult. We can easily skip the horoscope in the morning paper. Turning our eyes away from wickedness saves us from many dark places that leave painful scars on our souls.

By contrast, setting the good things God has provided before our eyes builds us up, refreshes us, and brings us light.

Father, in today's world, it's almost impossible to set no wicked thing before my eyes. TV, movies, billboards, and the internet all offer up impure images. Help me train my eyes to quickly look away when I come upon wicked images. Lead me in victory over the evil that stalks me. Help me as I search out that which is good and pure to set before my eyes.

Today's Takeaway

My eyes turn away from evil images.

I Dwell with the Faithful

Mine eyes shall be upon the faithful of the land, that they may dwell with me: he that walketh in a perfect way, he shall serve me.
Psalm 101:6

Who are our heroes? Who do we want to emulate?

To live a life pleasing to the Lord, we must hold the faithful of the land in esteem. We should dwell with those of like mind so they influence us positively as we do the same for them. That is how we become as lights to those who still walk in darkness.

Not only can we choose to "dwell" with the faithful of our generation, but we also can look to godly men and women of the past as role models. These devout individuals include Eric Liddell (*Chariots of Fire*), Jim and Elisabeth Elliot, William and Catherine Booth (Salvation Army), just to name a few—all faithful men and women of God and worthy of emulation.

Lord, there are many faithful men and women in the land. By your grace, I am numbered with them. The faithful are my brothers and sisters. With them, I walk in faith, serving and glorifying you.

Today's Takeaway

My role models are the faithful of the land.

God Listens to the Destitute

He will regard the prayer of the destitute, and not despise their prayer.
Psalm 102:17

The prayers of the destitute go to the head of the line. When we read the prayers of the Bible, including many offered up by David, the chief psalmist, we find almost universally that they are prayers of desperation from desperate people. They are prayers uttered by those with no other hope than the Lord. They know God will not despise their urgent pleas.

When our prayers are seemingly unanswered, one question to ask is "Am I truly desperate enough?"

Lord, you know when I am destitute and when I'm satisfied with the events of my life. I know that my satisfaction doesn't always result in powerful prayers, such as the desperate and destitute offer. My simple desire, then, is to have compassion on the destitute and join them in prayer for relief.

May we all put our hope and trust in you. God, hear the prayers of the destitute today.

Today's Takeaway

God is near in my desperation.

FUTURE GENERATIONS SHALL PRAISE HIM

But thou, O LORD, shall endure for ever; and thy remembrance unto all generations...
This shall be written for the generation to come: and the people which shall be created shall praise the LORD.

PSALM 102:12, 18

There are always people yet unborn—people to be created in the Lord's timing. For them, we pass along the testimony of a faithful God. Those who preceded us saw to it that their testimony was known and handed down to the next generation. Each new generation brings fresh testimonies to be shared in the future. Within families, there is a special blessedness when several generations have served the Lord, leaving the circle unbroken.

The goodness of the Creator is handed down from generation to generation, and yet it is always fresh to each new person conceived by God.

Father, how good it is to realize that you shall endure forever. All generations will remember you. Your Word shall also abide forever. Our heirs shall read about the same promises made to our ancestors. And, like the faithful who came before, we and our children and grandchildren will be blessed and praise you. There will never be a generation that doesn't praise you.

Today's Takeaway

God's promises are new for each coming generation.

This Earth Shall Perish

Of old hast thou laid the foundation of the earth:
and the heavens are the work of thy hands.
They shall perish, but thou shalt endure: yea, all of
them shall wax old like a garment; as a vesture shalt
thou change them, and they shall be changed:
But thou art the same, and thy years shall have no end.
Psalm 102:25-27

Someday all this that we see will perish. The mountains will crumble. The seas will recede. The planets will be no more. But despite those coming changes, God endures. He has no beginning, and he will have no end. The unchangeableness of our Creator assures our security. His promises also will endure through the coming ages.

Though all will eventually fail, our God remains forever. In him we have a firm hold on eternity.

Father, someday this present creation will perish, but you will forever remain the same. The ashes of the old creation fade away, but you will bring a new and better creation that will endure forever. Thank you for my eternal life that will someday live in that new incorruptible creation.

Today's Takeaway

All will one day perish...except God's truth.

Bless His Holy Name

Bless the Lord, O my soul: and all that is within me, bless his holy name.
Psalm 103:1

Names in Scripture are important. God has several important identifiers of himself. Included among his names are *El Shaddai* (Almighty God), *Adonai* (Lord), *Yahweh* (Jehovah), *Jehovah-Raah* (my Shepherd), *Jehovah Rapha* (the God Who Heals), *Jehovah Jireh* (the Lord Who Provides). There are more, of course, and a study of the names of God is spiritually profitable. Each name of God is evidence of His care for us: He is our shepherd, healer, provider, and Lord. At times, we may call on God by referring to one of his meaningful names. Whatever our need, the Lord is there for us.

Lord God, my all-sufficient one, my shepherd, healer, and provider, you are worthy of worship no matter which name I use—and in my distress, I will surely claim the name that fits my need. Thank you for giving us so many meaningful names by which to call on you and trust you. Today and always, you are my Jehovah Jireh, whatever my need.

Today's Takeaway

Every name of God is a blessing to us, and for those names, we bless his name.

ALL HIS BENEFITS

Bless the LORD, O my soul, and forget not all his benefits:
who forgiveth all thine iniquities; who healeth all thy diseases;
who redeemeth thy life from destruction; who crowneth
thee with lovingkindness and tender mercies;
who satisfieth thy mouth with good things; so that
thy youth is renewed like the eagle's.

PSALM 103:2-5

God does not prepare an unsatisfied life for us. He showers us with benefits and forgives the sins that weigh us down. He heals our diseases, redeems us from destruction, pours out his loving-kindness and tender mercies, and renews our youth. If we are dissatisfied with our lives, can it be traced to our not receiving the benefits he has prepared for us? God has invited us to a banqueting table. We need not look for food in alley dumpsters.

Father, you supply my every need. You invite me to forgo the dumpster for the banqueting table. Lord, I will not forget your benefits—the forgiveness of my sins, my redemption, your loving-kindness and tender mercies. Yes, Father, you satisfy me with all good things, and you even renew my fading youth. Praise your name!

Today's Takeaway

All of the benefits of being God's child are mine.

He Has Removed All My Transgressions

For as the heaven is high above the earth, so great is his mercy toward them that fear him.
As far as the east is from the west, so far hath he removed our transgressions from us.
Psalm 103:11-12

Many Christians are still weighed down by the remembrance of past sins, often because the repercussions of those sins still affect their lives. But the secret of moving past failures is to view them as God views them: as removed as far as the east is from the west. That's a distance that's literally impossible, yet it's the image God gives us to demonstrate just how free from our past sins he wants us to be.

Don't delay. Move ahead, no matter what your past sins were. They are indeed *past.*

Lord, why does this tape keep looping in my head that reminds me of past failures and sins? Why can't I, like you, forget my sins? After all, if you have forgiven me, my past sins carry no weight and thus should not be a burden to me. Help me, Father, replace that repetitious tape with a fresh recording of your promise of sins forgiven—and forgotten.

Today's Takeaway

I refuse to live my present life burdened by my past failures and sins.

We Are Dust

He knoweth our frame; he remembereth that we are dust.
Psalm 103:14

Sometimes we expect too much from ourselves. After all, we are dust. We are often weak, not up to the challenge of our present situation.

When this is the case, God knows. If we over-expect of ourselves, the Lord does not. He has sympathy with our dusty weakness and offers his strength, without accusation or condemnation.

Are you perhaps overloaded with situations that are too cumbersome for you? God would lift your heavy load. You were not made to bear that which a person made of dust cannot carry.

Though God remembers our dusty frames, we often do not.

O Lord, in a way it's refreshing to remember that I am but dust. Why should I, therefore, expect so much of myself—more than even you expect. Long ago we settled the fact that I am yours. What you do with me is up to you. I simply follow your lead and obey what I know to be your will. Father, thank you for knowing my flimsy frame. Thank you for showing me what I should do to lighten my burden.

Today's Takeaway

There is great joy in realizing my littleness before God.

The Earth Is Full of His Riches

O Lord, how manifold are thy works!
in wisdom hast thou made them all: the earth is full of thy riches.
Psalm 104:24

The Lord has made all we see (and all we don't see) in creation. Many of his manifold works are hidden, but they can be searched out by God-inspired men and women.

There remain cures for deadly diseases—we have just not yet uncovered that part of his riches. So many of our benefits today are the result of God putting the desire of discovery into the hearts of curious men and women. Such discoveries and inventions as electricity, photography, computerization, and certainly medical advances are all due to God's provision as revealed by inventive minds.

Lord, my life is rich with the benefits of inventions and advances made by others. And yet those benefits originate from you, not from man. You have provided the knowledge and opportunities for many good things we enjoy. How manifold, indeed, are your works. How full of riches, many yet undiscovered, is this earth. I pray you will lead the next generation of men and women who will uncover more secrets of your creation that will benefit mankind.

Today's Takeaway

Creation overflows with the wisdom of the Creator.
We need only to open our eyes.

His Glory Endures Forever

The glory of the Lord shall endure for ever:
the Lord shall rejoice in his works.
Psalm 104:31

How does God regard his works? He rejoices over them. What the Lord has done was announced as *good* in the very first days of creation. It is to God's glory that this universe and its inhabitants (us!) exist. And his glory is not like his creation, now fallen. Though this present creation will eventually dissolve, his glory will endure forever. The Lord will always rejoice in his works—and so must we.

O Lord, I join you in rejoicing over your works. This earth was created as "very good," but with the fall in the Garden of Eden it became corrupted. It shall soon pass away, but a new earth will follow. Even then, in the new and incorruptible world, there will be rejoicing. Even then, your glory shall endure forever. And even now your glory is a centerpiece to this world. We rejoice in your works!

Today's Takeaway

God rejoices over me!

A Lifetime of Singing His Praises

I will sing unto the LORD as long as I live: I will sing praise to my God while I have my being.

Psalm 104:33

Sometimes the healthiest thing we can do for our souls—and our bodies—is to rejoice in song. If we can make singing to the Lord our habit, we can overcome many inner hurts and disappointments. Our bodies respond positively when we adopt an attitude of praise. To live without a knowledge of God is to live on a lower plane. The higher plane is the plane of constant praise.

Make it your pledge that you will sing praise to God as long as you have being.

O God, you have created me, and for that alone, I praise you. Life with you is a happy existence because I have set the course of my life on a praise-filled track. While I have being—while I live—I live unto you. And I will sing praise as long as I exist.

Today's Takeaway

A lifetime of praise assures a satisfied life.

Sweet Meditation

My meditation of him shall be sweet: I will be glad in the Lord.

Psalm 104:34

David made a decision. He chose to be glad in the Lord. He purposed that his meditation of God would be sweet. He suffered much in his life, but he also had many joys. To sustain himself, he made the decision to be glad in the Lord. And that made all the difference.

It can make a difference for us too. We can have the sweet meditation of the Lord when we make the decision to be glad. You will be surprised at how joyfulness can change not only your heart but also your situation.

Be glad in the Lord today. Make that decision.

Lord, like David, may my meditation of you be sweet. May I daily take time to ponder your greatness. Give me, Father, a heart of gladness. I choose to rejoice in you no matter what tomorrow holds. Since you are my Lord and do not worry about what my tomorrow holds, neither, then, do I.

Today's Takeaway

Today and every day I will be glad in the Lord.

I Seek the Lord Daily

Seek the LORD, and his strength: seek his face evermore.
PSALM 105:4

God's strength doesn't come to us automatically. We must seek it. We must also seek his face—that is, seek *him* daily. For when we seek, we will find. If we do not seek, we do not find.

Many of us spend time pursuing the wrong things, or even good but lesser things. We seek finances, security, relationships, applause—the list is endless and unique to each of us. But we must remember the One who tells us to seek first the kingdom of God and his righteousness, and everything else we need will be given to us. That is a promise, and our calling as Christians is to live by the promises of God.

Today, are you living by the Lord's promises? Are you seeking his strength? His face? His kingdom?

Father, it's you and your strength I seek. Help me set aside all the cravings of my heart for lesser things—even good things that rival the best things. Assist me as I seek first your kingdom and righteousness, trusting that all I need will be added to me.

Today's Takeaway

Daily I seek the strength of the Lord.

The Favor of the Lord

Remember me, O Lord, with the favor that thou bearest unto thy people.

Psalm 106:4

Among the many blessings we have as the children of God is that of *favor*. Yes, the Lord marks out his beloved and gives them favor as needed. But with this approbation comes responsibility. We do not use privilege to bring acclaim to ourselves. Rather, this blessing is given that God might be glorified in whatever we do.

Is there a circumstance in your life that requires favor?

Ask God to remember you and grant you his kindness and support so he might be honored in the result.

Lord, you are the God who gives favor to your people. I know I have received your kindness even when I didn't recognize it as such. I pray for continued favor from you when the situation calls for it. I do not take your favor for granted, but I do claim it as a promise you have made to your people.

Today's Takeaway

God remembers me with favor.

Triumphing in His Praise

Save us, O Lord our God, and gather us from among the heathen, to give thanks unto thy holy name, and to triumph in thy praise.
Psalm 106:47

God gathers his children to himself. He assembles us from every nation—men, women, boys, and girls of every race. He gathers us to separate out a people for himself. We become the people of *his* pasture. This is all to the glory of his name.

Today, think of yourself as one God has called out from this world as his own. Give thanks to his holy name for being "gathered." Not all who are called respond—much to their own loss.

O Lord, how I praise you that I've been gathered "from among the heathen" to belong to you. I give thanks to your holy name. I pray now for my loved ones who have yet to be gathered into your sheepfold. Give them tender hearts that seek you and a hunger that can only be filled by you. Thank you for plucking us from this fallen world to be part of your eternal kingdom.

Today's Takeaway

I have been gathered for God. I rejoice and give thanks!

Praise Him

Oh that men would praise the LORD for his goodness, and for his wonderful works to the children of men!
Psalm 107:8, 15, 21, 31

So vital is praise to the psalmist that he repeats this exhortation four times in this one psalm.

It's astonishing that all people don't praise the Lord for his goodness. More surprising is the growing number of those who deny God's existence. Oh, what people miss when they can't break through the veil of unbelief and behold the God who created them and sustains them day by day—not to mention that they miss out on experiencing God's love.

Let us not be found with less praise than God deserves for his goodness and his wonderful works on our behalf.

How, Lord, can I convince others of your greatness? How can I urge them to praise you for your goodness? I can tell of your wonderful works, but will that convince them? Only you can reveal yourself to men and women in such a way that they seek you and praise you. Bring revival, O God, a revival of praise for your wonderful works.

Today's Takeaway

I praise God for his wonderful works!

The Lord Who Satisfies

For he satisfieth the longing soul, and filleth the hungry soul with goodness.
Psalm 107:9

Note that God does not satisfy every soul. He satisfies the *longing* soul. Nor does he fill the soul already full of itself. No, he fills the *hungry* soul—and that with goodness. When we long for God, he meets us with himself to fill that deep spiritual yearning.

How hungry are we for God? How deeply do we long for him? Are we willing to empty ourselves of whatever attractions this world has seduced us with? If so, we can be confident of his filling. He will not leave a longing soul unsatisfied, nor a hungry soul unfed.

Lord, my soul is indeed hungry for you. My very being longs for you. My desire is to be filled with the goodness you offer. I know I often also hunger after worldly things, much to my regret. I now put those aside and seek only you.

Fill me, Lord! Satisfy this longing soul.

Today's Takeaway

God satisfies my longing soul.

O to See His Wonders in the Deep

They that go down to the sea in ships, that do business in great waters; these see the works of the LORD, and his wonders in the deep.
PSALM 107:23-24

It was not those who hugged the safe shores that saw the works of the Lord. It was and is only those who venture out into the great and deep waters that will see God's magnificent works.

Determine that you will not be a shore-hugger, but that you will instead sail your ship into the deep waters and see the works of the Lord.

Lord, it looks safe close to the shore. I often want to stay there where the waters of the deep cannot overwhelm me. But then I know that your works are performed where the waters are deep. Only those few who are brave enough to venture far out, away from the shore, will see the wonders of the deep. Strengthen my heart, Father. Give me courage to let go of this safe and shallow shore and pursue you in the depths.

Today's Takeaway

If I want to experience God's wonders in the deep,
I must venture farther from shore.

My Desired Haven

He maketh the storm a calm, so that the waves thereof are still. Then are they glad because they be quiet; so he bringeth them unto their desired haven.
Psalm 107:29-30

We all have a desired haven that we seek as we venture home, away from the deep waters. Yes, we shall often visit the depths, but at other times God calls us to the harbor for rest. He sets our course for that safe moorage. We pass through storms along the way, but the Lord calms the waves.

He has determined that every child of his will enter their desired haven. We can peer off the ship's bow and see our haven far off…but coming ever closer by the minute. Soon we shall be there. What joy a respite will bring!

Lord, thank you for safe havens. Just as we have been in the depths together; so we come home to rest. Though we'll set sail again for the deep waters, let us enjoy the stillness and rest in the calm waters of home. May we be filled with gladness in the quiet. It is good to be home with you, Father, in my safe haven.

Today's Takeaway

I follow the Lord as he leads me to my desired haven.

Among the Nations

I will praise thee, O Lord, among the people: and I will sing praises unto thee among the nations. For thy mercy is great above the heavens: and thy truth reacheth unto the clouds. Be thou exalted, O God, above the heavens: and thy glory above all the earth.

Psalm 108:3-5

God is not bound to any particular nation, for his kingdom is not of this world. And yet he is to be praised in all nations. Why? Because his great mercy extends to all nations. His truth reaches the clouds. All men and women of every tribe and nation are invited to his table, but first they must hear of this glorious God. Thus the Lord calls his people either to become missionaries themselves or to support by prayer and finances those he sends to the nations. Spreading the good news of the gospel is an urgency we must all heed; thus will we sing unto God among the nations.

Lord, I do sing your praises among the nations. Your mercy is great among the heavens; your truth touches the clouds. Father, I do my part in reaching the nations with the knowledge of you and the good news that is the gospel. I pray for your messengers and do what I can to support them in prayer and finances. O Lord, be exalted among the people!

Today's Takeaway

I pray for the nations of the world to seek the Lord.

Deliver Thou Me

Do thou for me, O God the Lord, for thy name's sake:
because thy mercy is good, deliver thou me.

Psalm 109:21

Do we think we're imposing on the Lord when we ask him to "do for us"? If so, we're greatly mistaken. The truth is that the prayers God loves to answer usually begin with "Help!"

God is not reluctant to come to our aid. No, his mercy toward us is great. He delivers us, but he wants us to ask—to invite him into our situation. The sad alternative is to handle it ourselves. Never a good idea!

The Bible is full of people who boldly asked God to help them. Jesus encountered numerous individuals who were courageous enough to ask for his help, either through healing or in some other way. And help them he did. We, then, should not be shy in our asking: "Because thy mercy is good, deliver thou me!"

God, you invite me to ask you for help. So, yes, Father, please come in and "do thou for me." I know you will help because your mercy is great and because I see you move on behalf of those in the Bible who asked you for help. Thus will you deliver me too!

Today's Takeaway

The God who was faithful to men and women of the Bible
is also faithful to me.

His Mighty Hand Has Done It

Help me, O Lord my God: O save me according to thy mercy: that they may know that this is thy hand; that thou, Lord, hast done it.
Psalm 109:26-27

One of the reasons for God's seemingly last-minute rescues is that "they may know" the rescue was by his hand. Often even unbelievers see the work of the Lord and join us in acknowledging him.

"Help me, O Lord my God" is such a short prayer, but it says all that's necessary. It's a request for our God to intervene in our present situation. And because of his great mercy, he does help us in such a way so that we know it was his hand.

When the Israelites left their bondage in Egypt, God helped as they trekked toward the Promised Land. His hand was upon them, even when they couldn't see it. Likewise, the Lord responds to our cry for help, even if we don't see his answer right away.

His hand does the work—we respond with praise.

Lord, people are watching my life. They see my reactions to trouble and to good times. For them I pray as your merciful hand shapes the circumstances of my life.

Yes, O God, in the day of trouble, deliverance comes—and you, Lord, have "done it."

Today's Takeaway

God's blessings in my life are a testimony to others.

In the Day of Thy Power

Thy people shall be willing in the day of thy power, in the beauties of holiness from the womb of the morning: thou hast the dew of thy youth.

Psalm 110:3

It is the power of God that lives within us, moves us to divine action, fuels our prayers, establishes our victory. Do we rely on that power—his power—for our daily lives? If not, we are wasting time and energy.

Do we think God gives us power, expecting us to neglect it? No. God's power within us is there to enable us to live out his will. Thus, we see the many promises and examples in the Bible that portray the winning power of our Lord's strength.

Often that divine strength comes from our acknowledgment of our own weakness. It was the apostle Paul who understood that when he was weak, he was strong in God's strength.

O God, to the extent I've neglected your power within me, I repent. I regret the times I've relied on myself instead of relying on you. By faith, I live by the power of your Holy Spirit within me, and I echo the apostle Paul, who knew that his weakness paved the way for your strength.

Today's Takeaway

The power of the Holy Spirit resides in me.

We Have a Secure Covenant

He sent redemption unto his people: he hath commanded his covenant for ever: holy and reverend is his name. The fear of the Lord is the beginning of wisdom: a good understanding have all they that do his commandments: his praise endureth for ever.

Psalm 111:9-10

God saw our lost state and responded by sending his Son to redeem us from our sins and our sinful self. This he did by way of issuing a covenant, or testament. This covenant offers salvation and deliverance on God's end, and our part is to place our faith in that saving sacrifice. For wisdom, we rely on the fear of the Lord—the very beginning of wisdom.

We must note that God is not and cannot be a covenant breaker. His covenant with us is ironclad and forever. Reverend is his name.

Lord, you are a covenantal God. You have entered into a new and better agreement with your people: a covenant based on grace, not works, ratified by the shedding of Christ's blood on the cross. This covenant is mine forever—for you, O Lord, cannot break your covenant.

Today's Takeaway

God has invited me to be in covenant with him.

THE FEAR OF THE LORD BRINGS BLESSING

Praise ye the LORD. Blessed is the man that feareth the LORD, that delighteth greatly in his commandments.

PSALM 112:1

Do we want a blessed life? If so, the scriptural admonition is to fear the Lord and to delight greatly in his commandments. To do that requires leaving behind much of the advice the world offers about success.

Have you ever, even once, seen a book by an unbelieving author about fearing the Lord as a means to success? No, and you never will. For one thing, the world's definition of success is different than God's perspective. The idea of delighting in the Lord and his commandments is foreign to this world's way of thinking.

Put away the earthly success manuals and turn to God's Word. A good place to start is the book of Proverbs.

Lord, I want to succeed in life. I want to enjoy a blessed life. For that reason, I accept your word that fearing you and delighting in your commandments brings blessing. I turn away from this world's advice manuals that neglect fearing you as the means to success.

Today's Takeaway

Hidden within the fear of the Lord is a great blessing.

Favor, Grace in Action

A good man showeth favor, and lendeth:
he will guide his affairs with discretion.
Psalm 112:5

Guiding our affairs with discretion requires transparency and God's wisdom. In addition, we who would receive favor must also give favor when it's in our power to do so. Favor, like grace, is unmerited. It is grace in action.

When we receive favor, it is a grace offered to us. Likewise, when we show favor to others, we extend grace where it's not warranted.

We must also lend—with discretion—as God leads. Our assets are not our own. They, too, are "lent"—loaned to us by the Lord.

Father, I would be "good" and show favor by lending and by guiding my affairs with discretion. I will rely on your wisdom when it comes to exercising prudence.

You have shown me great favor; now may I likewise show favor to those who seek it.

Today's Takeaway

If I give, it shall be given unto me.

A Fixed Heart on Hearing Evil Tidings

He shall not be afraid of evil tidings: his heart is fixed, trusting in the LORD.
PSALM 112:7

Evil tidings naturally cause us to fear, to recoil, and perhaps even to go into denial. But what is God's way for us to receive bad news? He would remind us to have our hearts fixed on him in all circumstances. Though resolution of evil tidings may be slow in coming, we are to wait patiently, with our hearts fixed.

God never says, "Whoops, I didn't see that coming." The Lord knows about the evil tidings coming our way. He knows how each story will end. Our part is to keep our hearts fixed and to pray.

Rest assured that every situation, even the negative ones, will have God's desired end and we will ultimately benefit.

Lord, I do not like bad news. Sometimes I'm even fearful of evil tidings. But you remind me that I should not fear but should instead fix my heart, trusting in you. Help me to rejoice in all things—even as I receive troubling news.

Today's Takeaway

A fixed heart trumps evil tidings.

HIS NAME IS TO BE PRAISED

From the rising of the sun unto the going down of the same the LORD's name is to be praised.

PSALM 113:3

Why is God so insistent on receiving praise? Especially daylong praise? Truth be told, the rewards of praising our Creator are not just for his sake but also for *ours*.

When we actively praise God, either vocally or silently, we feel empowered. Why? Because our praise, being directed to the all-powerful One, redounds to us.

Worshipping God doesn't build him up—he's already full up.

No, glorifying God builds us up. If you doubt this truth, try it and see. Develop the praise habit, and your life will benefit greatly.

Lord, I do praise you daily. Though I'd worship you just for being who you are, I find I also benefit from actively praising you. My problem is I sometimes don't find words that glorify you as you should be glorified. I suspect the words I'm looking for don't even exist. Until I can praise you in eternity, I'll stick to the words I know, starting with "Hallelujah!"

Today's Takeaway

There is no time in the day or night when God is not to be praised.

God Raises the Poor and Lifts the Needy

He raiseth up the poor out of the dust, and
lifteth the needy out of the dunghill;
that he may set him with princes, even with the princes of his people.

Psalm 113:7-8

Who would ever consider lifting the poor and needy from the dunghill and setting them with princes? Who? God would. The Lord has a deep love for the needy—after all, he's our great need meeter. One might suspect God sets the poor with princes because he sees us all as royalty. And so we are.

Father God, I'm so glad that you prioritize the poor and needy. You bring them up high from their low estate. You crown them as royalty, and so they are. While the world often looks down on the poor and needy, you show compassion.

Lord, help me to always see the poor and needy the same way you do. I commit to helping those in need in any way I can. Lead me, God, in knowing my responsibility to your princes: the deprived and disadvantaged.

Today's Takeaway

When God rescues the poor and needy, they sit with royalty.

Trembling at His Presence

Tremble, thou earth, at the presence of the Lord,
at the presence of the God of Jacob;
which turned the rock into a standing water,
the flint into a fountain of waters.
Psalm 114:7-8

Our God is a glorious, mighty, miracle-working sovereign. He does what he wills—and his will is perfect.

His wondrous works cause us to tremble at his power. He who can bring water out of rocks sees our daily needs and provides for us, his people. We tremble not only at his power but perhaps more so that this awesome God cares for us as his beloved sheep.

We tremble, too, at his overpowering love for us. Who can comprehend such love? After all, we were once his enemies, and he loved us even then.

Lord, all the earth must tremble in your presence—as do I. You are the mighty God who brings water out of dry rocks and turns the flint into a fountain. You are the God of Jacob, and you are the God of me. I praise you, O Lord, for counting me among your sheep.

Today's Takeaway

I delight to tremble before the Lord my God.

Unto Thy Name Give Glory

Not unto us, O Lord, not unto us, but unto thy name give glory, for thy mercy, and for thy truth's sake.
Psalm 115:1

Wanting the notice of others—desiring glory for ourselves—is common to the natural man or woman. We are all to some degree glory seekers. But when we are walking in the Spirit, we reflect all glory to God and to him alone. Not unto us, never unto us, shall glory be given. If we are in a position to be noticed, commended, or flattered, we must never embrace the glory as our own. Like the scoring football players, we point up to heaven. He gets the glory for all our touchdowns.

O Lord, may it never be that I rob the honor due you. Make me, instead, a reflector of your glory. When others point to me in praise, I point up to you.

We both know the truth of the matter: Anything good coming from me has its origin in you. For the sake of all mercy and truth, unto your name do I give glory!

Today's Takeaway

Any glory I receive is reflected back to God.

He Is Mindful of Us

The LORD hath been mindful of us: he will bless us;
he will bless the house of Israel; he will bless the house of Aaron.
Psalm 115:12

Who can fathom a God so mighty and yet so mindful of sinful humanity? How can we understand the kind of love that brings blessings to a rebellious creation? How can he bless the house of one (Aaron) who led the people of God into worshipping the golden calf? How can he bless us, knowing our innermost thoughts?

The answer is that the Lord is merciful and full of grace. The old adage is true: Mercy doesn't give us what we deserve, and grace gives us what we don't deserve.

Lord, you are mindful of me. Amazing! Your blessing is even upon my house. I pray that the atmosphere in my home reminds visitors of you. I pray that in your mindfulness of me you would direct my path today. Show me your care throughout the day. Bring blessing into my life today. You are the Lord and giver of all blessings!

Today's Takeaway

My God is mindful of me and blesses me.

He Helps Those Who Are Brought Low

The LORD preserveth the simple: I was brought low, and he helped me.

Psalm 116:6

Who among us has not been brought low? Who has not been simple-minded? Who has not cried out to the Lord and received his help? *We all have.*

We all benefit from seeing ourselves as God sees us: simple, low, and helpless. Resist being proud, high, and self-sufficient. Those with that mindset will never see God at work. God is content to leave alone to their own devices those who see no need for the Lord's presence in their lives. They are the losers by their own choice.

Lord, just to be a simple Christian is my desire. I have been brought low, and you have lifted me up. You have always been my helper in tough times. In my simplicity, I often don't know what to do. But you always do.

When I cry out to you again, hear the plea of this simple child of yours. Rush to my aid as you would to a lamb caught in a thicket of briars.

Preserve me, O God.

Today's Takeaway

In my simplicity, the Lord blesses me.

The Lord Brings Rest to Our Soul

Return unto thy rest, O my soul; for the Lord hath dealt bountifully with thee.

Psalm 116:7

God does not give us a work list of projects we must do. In fact, he brings us to a place of deep rest. No works will get us into this rest. We enter this rest by faith. To be sure, there will be works to do, but they are the fruit of a soul at rest in God.

If striving has worn you down, it's time to stop the hustle and find rest for your soul. The works that follow will bear the best fruit.

Lord, I thank you that you're a God of bounty, not scarcity. You have created us to be receivers of your abundant grace and all-around provision. I have seen this in my own life during the times you have dealt bountifully with me. You have even provided a divine rest for me. From that place of rest, I fulfill your will for me. You grow the fruit of the Spirit in my life. Thank you, Lord, for both rest and bountiful blessings!

Today's Takeaway

God always deals bountifully with me.

No Fear of Death

Precious in the sight of the Lord is the death of his saints.
Psalm 116:15

Jesus wept at the death of Lazarus. Paul referred to death as an enemy. David wept over the loss of his infant son. No doubt Mary wept seeing her son tormented on the cross.

Death, though it comes to all of us, is nothing to be feared. God's remedy for our mortality was to have Christ overcome death through his death for us.

One day the victory at Calvary will be made fully clear for each of us. Now we see eternity from a distance. Until that day, we can know that the death of one of God's lambs is precious to him.

Knowing that, what have we to fear?

O God, if I look at my impending death through natural eyes, I'm fearful. But because of Christ, I can face it with victorious eyes. I can trust that the eternal life I now possess will see me ushered into your presence on my final day on earth. Most comforting is knowing that my death will be precious in your sight.

Today's Takeaway

God is moved by the death of those who love him.

His Truth Endures Forever

O praise the Lord, *all ye nations: praise him, all ye people.*
For his merciful kindness is great toward us: and
the truth of the Lord *endureth for ever.*
Praise ye the Lord.

Psalm 117:1-2

What would this world look like if all the nations praised the Lord? Every country would be at peace. Every population would experience his merciful kindness, and all would agree that his truth is *the* truth and will endure forever.

Such a hope in the face of the daily news seems impossible—and yet we should all pray and yearn for the kind of worldwide revival that would bring this dream to pass.

Lord, you are the God who brings revival in response to our prayers. And it is for revival that I do pray today. I ask you to bring about local, national, and even worldwide revival with the result that millions from all nations would rise up and offer praise to you. I pray that these millions would open their hearts to experience your merciful kindness and learn of your enduring truth.

O God, let it be so!

Today's Takeaway

I pray daily for a wave of revival to sweep the nations.

He Sets Me in a Large Place

I called upon the Lord in distress: the Lord answered me, and set me in a large place.

Psalm 118:5

The meadow in which God's sheep graze is not small and confined. Rather, our portion is large and plentiful. We may wander freely in the Lord's pasture, or we may simply rest beneath his mighty oaks.

Pity the Christian who never explores the large place God offers, who instead suffers in the narrow confinements of the barn stall. The best life has to offer is found not in the barn, not in the desert, not even in the forest, but in the lush green grass of our Lord's pasture.

Lord, I survey your land, and I see a wide expanse provided for your sheep. Every believer has a generous portion of this glorious meadow. I see green grass, flowing streams, gentle hills—a land of milk and honey. Your Word tells me that it's during distress, that when I call on you, you answer by setting me in this land of promise.

God, out of your riches, you give and give again to me. Praise your name!

Today's Takeaway

God has generously set me in a large place.

Man Can Do Nothing to Me

The Lord is on my side; I will not fear: what can man do unto me?
Psalm 118:6

Of our many fears, the fear of man is the most corrupt and the most needless of all. God is on our side. What does it matter who is on the other side? The Lord triumphs over all the foes of his people.

When the fear of man threatens, we can smile at the futility of it all. He who is on our side will not allow our enemy to harm us. Our true fear, after all, is not man, but rather it is God we fear—and that is the beginning of knowledge.

We must just make sure we are on the Lord's side.

Lord, when I feel threatened and tempted to fear what man can do to me, remind me that you are on my side, not on the side of those who oppose me. Man can do nothing of importance to me, for your power trumps any threats of humankind. Instead, I fear you and am thus wise and knowledgeable. And Lord, I am on your side...always.

Today's Takeaway

I fear no man, for the Lord is on my side.

Living to Declare the Works of the Lord

I shall not die, but live, and declare the works of the Lord.

Psalm 118:17

On any given day, we may breathe our last. We don't know when our move to heaven will occur. But until then, we *live*!

Are we making the most of each new day? Are we declaring the works of the Lord on our behalf, even if only to ourselves?

What is life for if it's not to know God, enjoy him, and make him known?

O God, I praise you for my life! I live and have my being as a gift from you. While I live, I will declare your works. While I live, I will embrace the chance to enjoy fellowship with you. No, Lord, I'm not ready to die. Give me, I pray, more days to declare your wonderful works!

Today's Takeaway

As long as I live, I shall declare the works of the Lord.

The Lord's Doing Is Marvelous

The stone which the builders refused is become
the head stone of the corner.
This is the LORD's doing; it is marvelous in our eyes.
PSALM 118:22-23

Of all people to write this psalm, David is the perfect choice. When Samuel called on Jesse to bring forth his sons so the next king of Israel might be known, Jesse brought them out one by one—except the least likely, David. Likewise, Jesus, rejected by his own people, is the very cornerstone of saving faith—a stumbling block.

Each one of us has felt overlooked at some point. The last one chosen for the sports team? The one not asked to the prom? The one passed over for a promotion?

Though we may know the sting of rejection, we must also know the end of the story: The rejected stone became the cornerstone. Our rejections, whether few or many, end at the gates of heaven.

Never be surprised at God's choices. He sees the heart. We do not.

Father, thank you that you do not refuse anyone who comes to you. After all, Jesus was rejected by his own people. He is still refused by the majority of the earth's population. Even so, you remain the God of rejects, the God of those who've been cast away. Such love is marvelous.

Today's Takeaway

There is no sting in rejection for me. Many of God's greatest heroes were rejected by the world.

Rejoicing in Today

This is the day which the Lord hath made;
we will rejoice and be glad in it.
Psalm 118:24

We have today, but for tomorrow we have only hope. None of us is guaranteed the next twenty-four hours. God, however, has given us *today*. It is ours to invest, to work, to play, to enjoy, to learn.

It's a day to rejoice and be glad since there will never be another day like today.

We may face a happy surprise, or we may hear bad news, but either way, we Christians can rejoice. God is with us to enjoy the ups and to comfort us in the downs.

O Lord, another day! Praise you for allowing me one more day in which to rejoice in you. No matter what today holds, it is a gift from you, and nothing can prevent me from being glad in it.

Today's Takeaway

I will always rejoice in another day custom-made by the Lord!

Heeding His Word Is Cleansing

Wherewithal shall a young man cleanse his way?
by taking heed thereto according to thy word.
Psalm 119:9

When we sin, where do we turn for cleansing?

The wrong and ineffective attempt at atoning for sin is to trust in good works to undo the damage inflicted by our offenses. We simply cannot work our way to righteousness. Nor can any ritual rid us of our sin. If works or rituals could have taken away our wrongdoings, then Christ died in vain.

Praise the Lord that there *is* a God-ordained way to be clean. We heed God's Word. We confess our transgression, repent, and, by faith, appropriate God's forgiveness. It's the same remedy for all who sin: men and women, old and young, smart and simple.

Lord, I have sinned. But there is cleansing from my offenses as I repent and claim your forgiveness by faith. I do not trust in good works or rituals to atone for my sins. Only trusting in Christ as my redeemer will cleanse me from sin.

Your Word strengthens me against my wrongdoings. As I obey, I move away from sinful tendencies. Father, may your cleansing fountain never run dry. May your Word keep me from sin.

Today's Takeaway

I cleanse my way by heeding God's Word.

God's Word Is a Refuge from Sin

Thy word have I hid in mine heart, that I might not sin against thee.
Psalm 119:11

One surefire way to overcome sin is to internalize God's Word. As the psalmist says, we *hide* the Word in our heart.

How do we do this? Memorizing helps. Pondering, meditating, slowly taking in the Word through careful reading—all of these are ways to help the Word of God penetrate our hearts and souls.

When tempted to sin, calling upon the hidden Word is an escape route out of danger and into victory. Find the verses and passages that are most effective for you when temptation strikes. Take that Word into your very being and use it as an antidote to the temptation.

God, though I have sinned, I know from your Word that I need not sin. How is this possible? By hiding your Word in my heart. Your Word is not a dead word. It is a living Word with power to save all who believe and to be a guardrail against sin.

Your Word, Lord, do I hide in my heart.

Today's Takeaway

I hide God's Word in my heart to overcome sin.

Wondrous Things Are in God's Law

Open thou mine eyes, that I may behold wondrous things out of thy law.
Psalm 119:18

Our eyes see so dimly the riches in God's law. The psalmist calls them "wondrous." But these treasures aren't visible to our earthly sight. Only when the Lord opens our eyes do we begin to marvel at God's secrets hidden in his Word.

Eyes closed to the things of God will never behold his wondrous things. Closed eyes blind us to truth. Open eyes bind us to truth.

It is a worthy prayer to ask God to "open mine eyes."

Without that prayer, the veil remains over the deepest secrets of the Lord.

Father, open my eyes! I so desire to behold the wondrous things in your law. Though they are not visible to my natural eyes, my spiritual eyes can see these sublime treasures that will surely change my life. Let me not close my eyes and thus miss your truth.

Teach me, Lord, from your Word. Show me wondrous things from your law.

Today's Takeaway

My eyes are open to behold wondrous things from God's law.

Choosing Truth

I have chosen the way of truth: thy judgments have I laid before me.

Psalm 119:30

God gives us many choices in life. The most important decision we make is which road in life will take us where the Lord wants us and where we'll find happiness.

Choosing the way of truth sets us off on a journey that cannot be unsuccessful. The road marked "Truth" is also called the highway of happiness. Every day we are able to make the same wise choice and move further down the road of God's plan for us.

When we stray, all is not lost. We can alter the bad choice we made and return to the pathway of truth, avoiding future distractions along the way and staying focused on the goal of a life well lived.

God, I have chosen the way of truth. I have laid your judgments before me. The way of lies I reject, though many others have chosen that path. To some, it appears alluring. But it leads to destruction. The narrower path of truth may not look as glitzy, but it's the way to a happy life.

Today's Takeaway

Daily I choose the way of God's truth.

Guard My Heart from Covetousness

Incline my heart unto thy testimonies, and not to covetousness.
Psalm 119:36

In a land of plenty, coveting is a natural response to seeing things we want. But God has promised to provide for us—and in so doing, he will not use our covetousness as his guide.

Set aside your desire for what your neighbor has. Turn away from wanting that colleague's job. Refuse to lust after another person's spouse. Be grateful for your friend's healthy bank account, but remember God is your source of all things. Let him decide.

Rather than wanting more, consider wanting less. Think about downsizing your excess goods and giving them to a ministry-run thrift store. That coat you never wear really belongs to the one who has no coat.

O Lord, I often see things I want for myself. To be honest, I have coveted things that are nicer than what I have. So, God, I do pray with the psalmist to incline my heart to your testimonies and away from covetousness. Help me be content with what I have and what you give me. I really don't need what others have.

Today's Takeaway

I resist the temptation to covet. I incline my heart to God's testimonies.

Turning Away from Vanity

Turn away mine eyes from beholding vanity;
and quicken thou me in thy way.
Psalm 119:37

Our days are best spent dealing with reality, not vanity. Vain desires are like vapor—they have no substance. Other people may chase the illusion, but we must walk according to truth.

The irony is that vanity is never satisfied. Once it becomes a motivator in our lives, it increases its hold on us. And when we're driven by self-love and conceit, we can't follow Christ on the road of the prized life, the road of humility.

Let God quicken us in our way with our eyes straight ahead, not turning to the arrogance and pride of vanity that flourishes in the natural world.

Lord, I see the contrast between the vanity of this world and the humility of your kingdom. I pray you would keep my eyes turned away from all vanity and instead focused on you. Quicken me in your way, O God, that I would stay on your path.

Today's Takeaway

I turn my eyes and my heart from the vanities of the world.

The Power of God's Word

Remember the word unto thy servant, upon
which thou hast caused me to hope.
This is my comfort in my affliction: for thy word hath quickened me.
Psalm 119:49-50

Where is hope found? It's in God's Word. When we need confidence and assurances, we open our Bibles and find the promise for the present need.

If we are afflicted, no matter the source of our trouble, the Scripture brings comfort. God's Word ushers life into any troubling situation. It also is a source of rejoicing during good times. There are, in fact, no circumstances in the events of our lives in which the Word of God cannot empower us.

When we have the comfort of God's Word, we have the presence and comfort of the Lord himself. *We have hope.*

Lord, your Word gives me hope. Remember, O God, the Word you give that brings comfort. When I am low, when I am in despair, your Word quickens me, and I once again have hope from you. This, then, is my comfort.

Today's Takeaway

God's Word has great power in my life. It comforts me in my affliction.

A Companion of the Righteous

I am a companion of all them that fear thee,
and of them that keep thy precepts.
Psalm 119:63

We become like those we spend the most time with. If we hang with the wrong crowd, we may find our spiritual life endangered. If we spend time with those who fear the Lord, however, we will surely be influenced for good. Best of all, let's be a companion of God. The more time we spend with him, the more we become like him.

Choosing godly companions will mean letting go of some longtime acquaintances. Truth be told, if we're living right, they may let *us* go.

How about this? Pray for new companions. Pray for God to send people into your life to help you in your Christian walk—or ones you can help on their journey.

Just know that you need not walk alone. Jesus knew this as he sent his disciples out two by two.

Lord, my greatest desire is to be more like you: more patient, compassionate, and forgiving. I do not want to be more like some of today's supposed role models: proud, angry, sassy, and loud. Lead me into deeper companionship with others who follow you and keep your precepts. Bring me faithful friends.

Today's Takeaway

I choose my closest companions from among the faithful.

God Does Good to Us

Thou art good, and doest good; teach me thy statutes.
Psalm 119:68

God is the source of all good—so much so that even the hard times we must go through have a redeeming value when entrusted to him.

What looks like disaster may be his blessing in disguise. Learn to look at life that way: The Lord is always at work to bring about good, either directly through blessing or indirectly through adversity.

Rejoicing in all things is what gets us through challenges. We must know beyond all doubt that God is good and does good. Without this assurance, when we go through a rough patch, we may be tempted to question the Creator's goodness—and that lets our enemy get a foot in the door to question God's goodness and to persuade us to become bitter.

Father God, you are the source of all good. You are, in fact, love itself. In becoming more like you, I desire to do good to others, especially anonymously. I pray you'll open my eyes to see ways to be Christlike to others. May I also learn to trust that during adversity you're behind the scenes working for my ultimate good.

Today's Takeaway

God is my teacher in that which is important.
He is good and does good!

LEARNING FROM MY AFFLICTIONS

It is good for me that I have been afflicted; that I might learn thy statutes.
PSALM 119:71

Through affliction, unpleasant that it might be, we learn to trust God in the process. We learn more of his ways. When we have passed through tribulation and come out on the other side, we can more clearly see the plan of the Lord.

How it would change our lives for the better if we welcomed affliction as though it was a great teacher, sent to instruct us in life. But being human, our natural response to hardship and heartache is to pray it away. And that's okay, as long as we also learn the lesson of affliction. As the psalmist notes, the lesson is learning our Creator's statutes—his principles for a better life.

God, truth be known, I'm not a fan of affliction. And yet tribulation does seem to find me—sometimes when I least expect it. Lord, you can help me change my attitude. I know you don't ask me to seek affliction, but you ask me to learn from it. Open my eyes to see the lesson of each hardship—even as I pray for its removal from my life.

Today's Takeaway

When afflicted, I look for the good to come of it.

God's Word Is Unchanging

For ever, O Lord, thy word is settled in heaven.
Psalm 119:89

In this life almost everything is subject to change—everything, that is, except God and his Word, which are settled forever in heaven and on earth. It's the one constant we have in a very unconstant world.

It's awesome to consider that God's Word not only guides us today but also gave spiritual life to the great Christians of the past: Jonathan Edwards, Hannah Whitall Smith, Oswald Chambers, and many more. Just think of the work the settled Word of God did in their lives and consider what it can do in each of our lives.

So rely fully on God's Word. It is the rock on which we stand, high above the swirling waters below. It is the settled way of life for each of us.

God, I live in an unsettled world. Changes happen that worry me. What does the future hold? Wars? Earthquakes? Fires? Floods? And what of personal relationships that once seemed stable but now I'm not so sure about? Oh, the joy of having your settled Word in this crazy world.

Today's Takeaway

God's Word is forever settled.

MEDITATING ON GOD'S LAW

O how love I thy law! it is my meditation all the day.
PSALM 119:97

God's law was so important in David's life that he meditated on it throughout the day. We can do likewise—if we learn to love the Lord's law as David did.

Elsewhere in Scripture we're told that "thou wilt keep him in perfect peace, whose mind is stayed on thee" (Isaiah 26:3). The recipe for a happy life is found in making God and his Word and his law the center of our life. Consequently, the recipe for a failed life is to ignore the Lord's laws and principles and go our own way.

Goodness and mercy follow the lovers of God's law. Sadness and disappointment are the lot of those who ignore his instructions.

Lord, your law is sweet to me. As I meditate on it, I'm blessed, for your law instructs me in the way I should go. It keeps me on the right path and is my source of wisdom.

When I'm hungry, I find food. When I'm spiritually hungry, I meditate on your Word.

Today's Takeaway

I love God's law. It is perfect, though I am imperfect.

The Avoidance of Evil

I have refrained my feet from every evil way, that I might keep thy word.
Psalm 119:101

Our feet can take us places we don't want to go—if we let them. Keeping our feet from treading toward evil is as important as keeping our eyes from viewing evil or our mouth from speaking evil.

David had a choice as to where his feet would take him. We have that same choice. Wise is the Christian who knows how to keep God's Word and how to restrain his or her feet from every evil way.

But not only must we keep our feet from every evil way, we also must plant our feet on every firm and godly path before us. Saying no to evil is accomplished by also saying yes to righteousness.

Lord, the footprints of the lost lead to a tragic end. Like them, I'm often tempted. But I have learned a lesson by watching the fallen as I keep your Word. Sometimes my feet want to follow my erring friends, but I make the final choice as to where my feet go—and that's to follow the footprints of my fellow believers who also strive to keep your Word.

Today's Takeaway

To avoid sin, I am careful where my feet take me.

The Sweetness of God's Word

How sweet are thy words unto my taste! yea,
sweeter than honey to my mouth!
Through thy precepts I get understanding: therefore I hate every false way.
Psalm 119:103-104

Some people mistake God's words as cumbersome, inconvenient, or old-fashioned. They may even make the error of calling his words "bitter."

The truth is that God's words taste sweet to lovers of our Lord. Thus consuming God's words is pleasant, even joyful. It's the absence of God's words that is bitter, leading us into confusion and error. It beckons us on to the false ways that are destructive and counter to God's truth.

Be safe by tasting the Lord's sweet words today. They are like a lavish dessert after a fine meal. Turn away from every false way.

Lord, I love your Word—and your words. I find them sweet to the taste; they refresh and delight me. Your words give me understanding for my life. Your precepts are guideposts along the way.

Truth is the treasure I seek; therefore, I hate every false way that would lead me off your chosen path for me.

Today's Takeaway

Through God's precepts, I get understanding,
and I hate every false way.

Vain Thoughts

I hate vain thoughts: but thy law do I love.
Psalm 119:113

Vain thoughts are thoughts that take us nowhere: notions of self, empty visions of what we think ought to be or what we ought to have that isn't ours. We can easily build a fantasy world where all revolves around us. These conceited notions are at war with thoughts of a renewed Christian mind. They question God's Word and rationalize away all righteous reasoning in order to maintain the illusory world of vain thoughts that delay our destiny with the Lord. If we accept vain thoughts and continue in them, we have no one to blame but ourselves for the result.

Lord, sometimes my thoughts are scattered. I then must reel them in and discipline my mind. I must reject vain thoughts that aren't based on reality. My reflections must be aligned with your perfect law so I can enjoy the life you've given me. Help me, Father, to have the mind of Christ. May godly thoughts guide my life.

Today's Takeaway

Vain thoughts are not welcome in my mind.
God's law is more than welcome.

ORDERED STEPS

Order my steps in thy word: and let not any iniquity have dominion over me.
PSALM 119:133

When our steps are in accord with God's Word, we are more resistant to the sins that want to dominate us. It's right to pray that God would not allow any iniquity to have dominion over us. It's even better to pray that righteousness would reign in our lives.

What sins or proclivities to sinful behavior lie at your door? Quickly dispatch them with the assurance that God answers prayers for deliverance from iniquity. Enjoy the peace that comes from walking in steps ordered by the Word of God. Allow God's Holy Spirit to have dominion over you.

Lord, when iniquity—sin—comes knocking on my door, help me to order my response according to your Word. Without that protection, sin would surely have dominion over me. Yes, Father, order my steps in keeping with your Word. May your Holy Spirit have dominion over me.

Today's Takeaway

I refuse to allow any iniquity to have dominion over me.

The Nearness of God

Thou art near, O Lord; and all thy commandments are truth.
Psalm 119:151

When we were children, we may have imagined God as "up there" in heaven. We could visualize him on his throne, high in heaven, his long white beard flowing. But as adults, we know that God is always near. It's impossible to flee from his presence. He is near now, as you read this. You can reach out and touch him with your prayers, and he will hear. He knows your need, and he's here to supply you with strength for each new day, one at a time.

Forget the childish notion of the Lord being far away. Draw near to God and he will draw near to you.

God, I thank you that I long ago outgrew the childish image of you with the long white flowing beard. What an erroneous picture! You cannot be described as one who is infirm with age. Nor are you far away in outer space. You are near. You are here. Your truth is here and available to me and to all who seek you. Praise your name, most holy God!

Today's Takeaway

God is near—never far from me.

The Happiness of Great Peace

Great peace have they which love thy law: and nothing shall offend them.
Psalm 119:165

In a world with ascending suicide rates and evening newscasts that would scare the devil himself, it's important to remember that we are immune from the fears that accompany all that tragedy and heartache. We who love God's law have great peace, regardless of circumstances.

Nothing shakes us, nothing offends us. If anything, when the news reports are troubling, we cling even more closely to the Lord of all peace.

The promise of great peace is to all who love God's law. Love his law and experience abiding tranquility beyond understanding.

Father, I live in a world where many do not experience great peace. Though this serenity isn't hidden—it's open to all—few seem to find it or even search for it. I'm thankful that I've found this great peace. Help me, then, Lord, to share your enduring peace with the fearful.

Today's Takeaway

Because I love God's law, I enjoy great peace.

Desiring Peace

I am for peace: but when I speak, they are for war.
Psalm 120:7

Jesus, in his Sermon on the Mount, declared, "Blessed are the peacemakers" (Matthew 5:9). God desires peace for his people—not war, violence, and death. Certain situations arise that call for war, but that's due to the nature of man, not the nature of God. Every Christian should pray for peace and work toward that end. We should never be the instigators of violence. Peter learned this the hard way. He thought he was doing right by taking up his sword and cutting off the ear of Malchus, one of the servants of the high priest. But Jesus told Peter, "Put up again thy sword into his place: for all they that take the sword shall perish with the sword" (Matthew 26:52).

Lord, I am a peaceful person. I don't like conflict, whether interpersonal or global. It's easy to escape responsibility by invoking the time-worn cliché "What can one person do?" But I'm that one person, Father. I can surely pray for peace in my life. I can pray for the victims of violence. I can pray against bullying nations that provoke tragic wars. And I can give time or money to responsible Christian ministries that work for peace and that aid innocent victims of war.

Today's Takeaway

I work and pray for peace. I practice peace with those I know.

Our God Never Sleeps

He will not suffer thy foot to be moved:
he that keepeth thee will not slumber.
Behold, he that keepeth Israel shall neither slumber nor sleep.
Psalm 121:3-4

God is always there and always here. We cannot be moved out of his care. He never takes his eyes off us because he never needs sleep. He is our 24-7 God, and we are his 24-7 children. In keeping watch over us, he observes our situations, hears our cries, and loves our praises. And just as he is constantly concerned with us, so should we always be aware of him and his concerns. As Jesus said, "Thou shalt love the Lord thy God with all thy heart, and with all thy soul, and with all thy mind" (Matthew 22:37). That's a 24-7 love on our part.

Dear Lord, one aspect of your being is your omnipresence. You are always here, just as you are always there. There is no place you are not. There is no time when you are absent from governing the universe. Your eyes are always upon me, your attention focused on me…even when I'm unaware. Lord, you steady me. You keep my feet from being moved. You have made me the object of your love.

Thank you, Father, for your ever-presence!

Today's Takeaway

I cannot be moved. God is always watching over me.

The Joys of the House of the Lord

I was glad when they said unto me, Let us go into the house of the Lord.
Psalm 122:1

The first of two joys of being a Christian is that we have a home in the house of the Lord where we are always welcome. The doormat is always out.

The second joy is that when we're in the house of the Lord, we're never alone. Our heavenly Father is there, and so are his other children, our brothers and sisters in Christ.

When we were children, some of us were taught that the church building was God's house, but in truth, his house is much larger than any building. The true house of the Lord is where his people are gathered in his name—and that's where we long to be.

What a fellowship we have in loving God and each other, and in resting in the house of the Lord.

Pure gladness!

Lord, how I love to dwell in your presence, in your house. How I love to be with your people—my people, too, since they are my brothers and sisters in Christ. The joy in your house is never-ending. Sadness cannot gain entrance to your house.

O Father, bring others into your house. There's plenty of room!

Today's Takeaway

The house of the Lord is always open to me (and to others!).

My Eyes Are Trained on the Lord

Unto thee lift I up mine eyes, O thou that dwellest in the heavens. Behold, as the eyes of servants look unto the hand of their masters, and as the eyes of a maiden unto the hand of her mistress; so our eyes wait upon the LORD our God, until that he have mercy upon us.

PSALM 123:1-2

When our eyes are trained on the Lord, we see all things clearly. We look to him and see his love for us in his eyes. We are his glad servants and wait upon him for direction, eager to please him who provides so well for us.

If your gaze has drifted away from him, lift up your eyes to behold him in all his glory.

Fix your gaze on your Master.

Father, my eyes are fixed on you. Like a good servant watches for, and even anticipates, the needs of the master, so do I train my eyes on you. I wait upon you with pleasure and am always ready to obey your directives. If my eyes should wander, please remind me through your Spirit to return my attention to you, for you have always turned your attention toward me.

Today's Takeaway

I fix my eyes fast on God.

The Snare Set for Me Is Broken

Blessed be the LORD, who hath not given us as a prey to their teeth.
Our soul is escaped as a bird out of the snare of the
fowlers: the snare is broken, and we are escaped.
Our help is in the name of the LORD, who made heaven and earth.
PSALM 124:6-8

Dare we ever forget the snare that once held us captive? It's good to recall where we've come from and who it was that set us free from the enemy's trap. Now released, we are determined to help others escape the snare of the fowler. And how do we lead others to freedom? Evangelism. Though many are captives, few are the messengers of freedom. Watch today and see if God has arranged a divine appointment for you to share the good news of the gospel.

God, you have set me free from sin, from the enemy of my soul, and from even myself. Now help me be a messenger of your deliverance. Many are caught in the snare of the fowler and would welcome freedom if they only knew how to escape. I am an example, Lord. Give me the opportunities and the words to bring your deliverance to the captives.

Today's Takeaway

Having been freed from the fowler's snare,
I will not be taken captive again.

I Am Unmovable

They that trust in the Lord shall be as mount Zion,
which cannot be removed, but abideth for ever.
As the mountains are round about Jerusalem,
so the Lord is round about his people from henceforth even for ever.
Psalm 125:1-2

On days when we feel weak and movable, we must remember that when we trust in God, we are as a mountain that *cannot* be removed. This is a promise from God himself. Emotions are good when they follow the Lord's truth, but they can be deceptive and fleeting when they try to lead, not follow.

By faith (apart from feelings) we shall abide forever with the protective hand of God surrounding us. We are unmovable not only now but also eternally.

We are firmly *his*.

Praise you, Lord, I am immovable! Though there are many temptations that would move me, I refuse them all. I trust in your Word that promises you will be round about me as the mountains are around Jerusalem. I stand strong in you, my God!

Today's Takeaway

I am as immovable as the highest mountain.

Reaping in Joy

They that sow in tears shall reap in joy.
He that goeth forth and weepeth, bearing precious seed, shall doubtless come again with rejoicing, bringing his sheaves with him.
Psalm 126:5-6

As we shed our tears, we often fail to see the outcome from God's perspective. Yes, we cry, but with our tears is precious seed that, when sprouted, will see our tears not of pain but of joy. We shall bring forth a full harvest, sheaves without number.

Lord, I know that to have a good crop, one must start with good seed. You have given me "precious" seed. Though my tears must fall, they water the sprouting seeds, and soon I will reap a hearty crop.

Today's Takeaway

"Everything is preparation for something else. Every story is part of a larger story. Every event, regardless of whether it seems good or bad, is a seed planted, watered, sprouted, or readied for harvest."

—Chuck Smith

The Lord Is the Builder of the House

Except the Lord build the house, they labor in vain that build it: except the Lord keep the city, the watchman waketh but in vain.

Psalm 127:1

We've all seen buildings reduced to rubble. We've seen the result of structures without a firm foundation. Such is the fruit of man's workmanship. Even if the tattered building has lasted a hundred years, it will eventually fall.

But not if God is the builder. Not if there is a firm foundation. Whatever we build, it is to be built by the Lord working through us. We still labor, but with God's power in us.

The foundation of any work is the sure Word of God.

Without the Lord, without a good foundation, the building will fall. Likewise, if we "keep the city," it, too, is in vain. It is God and God alone who is at work building the house, keeping the city, bringing forth good fruit through us.

Dear Lord, you are the builder, not me. My workmanship is shoddy at best. The house is condemned as soon as the last nail is in place. The foundation gives way, and my labor is in vain.

You are the keeper of the city. You watch over us with care. Your eyes never depart from us.

Today's Takeaway

My spiritual life has been crafted by God himself, so it will stand.

He Giveth Sleep

It is vain for you to rise up early, to sit up late,
to eat the bread of sorrows: for so he giveth his beloved sleep.
Psalm 127:2

Many of us know the futility of trying to fall asleep without success. It may be our minds are busy with tomorrow's agenda. It could be family worries. Or health issues. Or we might be eating the bread of sorrows.

We've tried warm milk, taken sleeping pills that leave us groggy in the morning, and perhaps even resorted to counting sheep.

At some point we must simply rely on the Lord to bring restful sleep. So at rest are we to be that we enter easily into the sleep God gives us. What good does it do to eat the bread of sorrows, turning sleeplessly on our beds?

All such worry is in vain. It is he that gives us true rest. Make your final thoughts of God and his promises for sleep. Rehearse his many blessings. We trust him for wakefulness—we must also trust him for sleep.

When my troubles keep me awake, I know it's time to rest in you and let you give me sound sleep. The bread of sorrows has a bitter taste. Sweeter is the living bread you feed me.

Lord, bring rest and sweet sleep.

Today's Takeaway

God gives rest during the day and sweet sleep at night.

A Quiver Full of Arrows

Lo, children are an heritage of the Lord: and
the fruit of the womb is his reward.
As arrows are in the hand of a mighty man; so are children of the youth.
Happy is the man that hath his quiver full of them: they shall not
be ashamed, but they shall speak with the enemies in the gate.

Psalm 127:3-5

Children are blessings from God. A mighty man carries many arrows in his quiver for the fight before him. So, too, does the Christian rely on a quiver full of children to meet the "enemies in the gate." Be thankful for the Lord's provision for the strength of many arrows.

Lord, there is a battle to be waged...and won. I do not have to fight this war alone though. You provide my children as arrows in my quiver; thus, I am fully armed for battle. Even those without children have the arrows of other youth to come to their aid. The body of Christ is full of arrows fit for spiritual battle when called upon. Happy then are all who have their quivers full.

Today's Takeaway

My quiver is full of arrows in the persons of my family
and brothers and sisters in Christ.

It Shall Be Well with Me

Blessed is every one that feareth the LORD; that walketh in his ways. For thou shalt eat the labor of thine hands: happy shalt thou be, and it shall be well with thee.

Psalm 128:1-2

If we would enjoy a blessed life, we must fear the Lord and walk in his ways—even when those ways are not our natural ways. To fear the Lord and walk in his ways, we must be men and women of God's Word. Where else would we learn his ways?

We are all called to a work with our name on it. When we're faithful to that divine assignment, we will find happiness, and "it shall be well with thee." It does no good to avoid our assignment. Just ask Jonah how that goes.

God, you want the best for me. You want me to be blessed. For this reason, you show me your ways and how to walk in them. You teach me how to fear you. You give me a field of labor so that I will find fullness and happiness. I rest on your promise that it shall be well with me.

Today's Takeaway

God has decreed that it shall go well with me. I trust him.

The Fate of the Wicked

The LORD is righteous: he hath cut asunder the cords of the wicked.
Psalm 129:4

When we're in the grips of temptation or in any way influenced by the wicked one, we can turn to the Lord and see him, our righteous God, cut asunder the cords that have us bound.

We need never fear Satan's minions when our Creator is at the center of our life. We easily triumph over the evil one and all his strangling cords. Where he sows seeds of cursing, God sows seeds of blessing that bear good fruit. We must learn to discern the wicked one's tactics and resist them.

Father, evil still exists in this world. The wicked are still at large and under the command of Satan. But you, Lord, are altogether righteous. You have cut asunder the cords the evil one has with my name on them. He cannot prevail in his plans to destroy me when you have plans to prosper me and bless me. How I praise you for my victory over the wicked one.

Today's Takeaway

God has negated the attacks of the enemy
by cutting asunder his cords.

Iniquity? Yes. Forgiven? Yes!

If thou, Lord, shouldest mark iniquities, O Lord, who shall stand?
But there is forgiveness with thee, that thou mayest be feared.
Psalm 130:3-4

The Bible reminds us that all have sinned and come short of the glory of God. And if God were to take into account our many iniquities, none of us could stand before him. If we were struck by lightning bolts for our sins, none of us would survive. But, praise God, there is the forgiveness of our transgressions through the shed blood of Christ. We have no fear of judgment for our sins. Our only fear is the righteous fear of God.

Thank you, Lord, that there is forgiveness with you. Gladly do I fear you—my redeemer. While my sins were many, your forgiving nature sought out my iniquities and forgave them. If you had not done so, I would not be able to stand before you. Blessed be your name, Jehovah Jireh, *my provider.*

—∞—

Today's Takeaway

I live as a forgiven Christian.
No sin from my past has any power over me.

As a Child That Is Weaned

Lord, my heart is not haughty, nor mine eyes lofty:
neither do I exercise myself in great matters, or in things too high for me.
Surely I have behaved and quieted myself, as a child that is
weaned of his mother: my soul is even as a weaned child.

Psalm 131:1-2

Humility is the hallmark of the Christian. We of all people know that we're unworthy of all God has provided for us, and we are thankful. Plus, we have the perfect role model of humility in Jesus Christ.

Our faith does not lend itself to haughty eyes or in thinking great thoughts of ourselves. We're content to be who God made us—not anxious over who we are not. We are childlike in our contentment, quieted and satisfied in God's portion for us.

O Lord, may I simply be used by you in whatever capacity you choose. Large or small, whatever talents I have are yours. When I see the wrong kind of pride in my life, help me reject it and put on the humility of Christ.

Today's Takeaway

My heart is not haughty; my soul is as a weaned child.

Shout for Joy

Arise, O Lord, into thy rest; thou, and the ark of thy strength.
Let thy priests be clothed with righteousness;
and let thy saints shout for joy.
Psalm 132:8-9

We who are believers in Christ are "saints." The word has the connotation of being set apart for God's purpose, and so we are. We are also priests, according to the apostle Paul. As priests, we are righteous with the righteousness of Christ.

So astonished are we by God's goodness to us that we shout for joy. We cannot be silent when the Creator is blessing us—and even more so when he is using us for his kingdom. How can we not then shout for joy?

God, you have clothed me with the righteousness of Christ; therefore, I rejoice in you. I shout for joy. Arise, O Lord. You are my strength. You have made me a priest, and in that role, I pray for wisdom and the necessary discernment for the assignments you have for me.

Today's Takeaway

God's call is a call to separation.

Brotherly Unity

Behold, how good and how pleasant it is for
brethren to dwell together in unity!
It is like the precious ointment upon the head, that ran down upon the beard, even Aaron's beard: that went down to the skirts of his garments;
as the dew of Hermon, and as the dew that descended
upon the mountains of Zion: for there the LORD
commanded the blessing, even life for evermore.

Psalm 133:1-3

Where unity under God is evidenced, the Lord commands a blessing. Our Father's will is always for his children to dwell together in harmony. When division comes in, the blessing of God goes out. It's up to each of us to be in one accord with our fellow believers. We are members of one family, with God as our Father.

Lord, you are my Father and the Father of my many brothers and sisters in Christ. I thank you for each of my siblings. Though we may disagree on minor issues, we are united in our saving faith in Christ. I hold my opinions on certain topics with care, realizing I might be wrong in some of the debatable issues—and what a tragedy to lose fellowship over something either I or my brother or sister was mistaken about. Above all, let me never raise my voice in anger over my kin in Christ. My raised voice is reserved for your praises.

Today's Takeaway

I am in unity with all my brothers and sisters in Christ.

Lift Up Your Hands

Behold, bless ye the Lord, all ye servants of the Lord,
which by night stand in the house of the Lord.
Lift up your hands in the sanctuary, and bless the Lord.
The Lord that made heaven and earth bless thee out of Zion.

Psalm 134:1-3

It is no chore to bless the Lord. It is our privilege to stand in awe before God, to lift our hands in worship and verbally praise him. It is he who made heaven and earth. It is he who has made each of us and called us to be his beloved sheep.

Lift your hands then. Bless the Lord today. He is worthy!

O God, I lift my hands to you as a sign of my surrender and praise. As a servant, it's only fitting that I show my surrender—not just with my hands but also with my heart. So today I raise my hands in worship to you, the Lord who made heaven and earth, remembering Christ who lifted his arms on the cross for me.

Today's Takeaway

I lift my hands to bless the Lord!

Pleasant Praises

Praise ye the Lord. Praise ye the name of the Lord;
praise him, O ye servants of the Lord.
Ye that stand in the house of the Lord, in
the courts of the house of our God.
Praise the Lord; for the Lord is good: sing
praises unto his name; for it is pleasant.
Psalm 135:1-3

When we're faced with unexpected unpleasantness, it's good to remember the pleasant joy of singing praises to God in the midst of our circumstances. Praise has a way of dispelling the unpleasantness of any troubling situation.

The apostle Paul sang God's praises in prison. Can we who are free from our shackles of sin do less? Can we who are God's servants refuse to praise our Master?

Sing praises to God today, no matter what the day holds.

O Lord, it is indeed pleasant to sing your praises, for you are good. You bring good into my life, and when bad makes its entrance, you eventually make it all right. Today I worship you, whatever comes my way. My praises declare my trust in you!

Today's Takeaway

I'm a servant who daily praises my Master.

I Shall Never Trust in the Idols of Man

The idols of the heathen are silver and gold, the work of men's hands.
They have mouths, but they speak not; eyes have they, but they see not;
they have ears, but they hear not; neither is
there any breath in their mouths.
They that make them are like unto them: so
is every one that trusteth in them.

Psalm 135:15-18

When we came to Christ, we set aside our previous idols, whether they were actual graven idols or the false gods of riches, fame, ambition, or sensuality.

There's no shortage of possible idols any one of us might have worshipped. But when we came to realize how foolish and empty those false gods were—and how very like them we have been—it was obvious we needed to relinquish false idols and turn our worship to the true God, never again looking back to our days in darkness.

We are of the light now.

Lord, I thank you that all my idols are gone. I no longer bow down to them, nor do I worship them, for they have no power—they are futile for all purposes. You are now my counselor, redeemer, and Lord.

Today's Takeaway

I live in God's light, having left my idols in their darkness.

His Mercy Endures Forever

O give thanks unto the LORD; for he is good: for his mercy endureth for ever.

PSALM 136:1

In each of the twenty-six verses of this psalm, the psalmist gives us a reason to give thanks to the Lord. And each verse ends with the reason for giving thanks: His mercy endures forever.

So then must our praise endure forever.

Although we give thanks verbally, we can also show our thanks by our actions. Today you may have an opportunity to help someone and receive their thanks. Let it be a reminder of our giving of thanks to our Lord Jesus, who deserves our endless gratitude for redeeming us.

O Lord, surely it was because other words failed to thank you enough that the psalmist felt he could only repeat his thanks for your goodness and your everlasting mercy. Like him, I'm at a loss for any other words. So, too, do I repeat my thanks. May it, also, endure forever.

Today's Takeaway

My praises to God endure forever because his mercies endure forever.

I Will Sing of the Lord in This Strange Land

How shall we sing the LORD's song in a strange land?
Psalm 137:4

When the Israelites were in captivity, they were hard-pressed to sing God's praises. It's easy to praise God in a friendly land. But while enslaved? And yet it's when we're in captivity that we most need to sing our praises to our Creator. Certainly, the apostle Paul would concur, having sung God's praises while he was literally captive in prison.

Are you a prisoner in a strange land now? Then sing his praises. Sing as if you are no longer held captive. Truth be told, singing his praises will bring about your freedom.

Lord, I sing your praises in both strange and familiar lands. I've known captivity and I've known freedom. Wherever I am, your praises are with me, freeing me. If anything, the praises in captivity taught me that I can be free under all circumstances. And that praise in a strange land leads me on the path to my familiar homeland. Thus will I praise you at all times and in all places.

Today's Takeaway

I will sing of the Lord in this strange pre-heaven world.
How can I not?

My God Strengthens Me

I will praise thee with my whole heart: before
the gods will I sing praise unto thee...
In the day when I cried thou answeredst me, and
strengthenedst me with strength in my soul.
Psalm 138:1, 3

There are days, weeks—perhaps even months—when we feel weak, desiring strength we don't have. During such rough patches, we must cry out all the more to God and know he will answer by strengthening our souls. If we fail to cry out, we will continue in weakness.

But note that the psalmist was a praiser of God with his *whole* heart. God does not need nor does he deserve halfhearted praise.

When you call out to the Lord for strength, make sure it's a wholehearted cry.

O God, you are the one who hears me when I cry out to you. You strengthen me in my soul so that I can go through any trial or tribulation. No human or demonic strategy can defeat me when my soul is empowered with your strength. May my every cry result in yet greater strength.

Today's Takeaway

My cries to God are wholehearted, not weak or half-hearted cries.

God Takes Note of the Lowly; Not So the Proud

Though the Lord *be high, yet hath he respect unto the lowly: but the proud he knoweth afar off. Though I walk in the midst of trouble, thou wilt revive me: thou shalt stretch forth thine hand against the wrath of mine enemies, and thy right hand shall save me.*

Psalm 138:6-7

If we would be known by God, we must realize our lowly estate. If pride is our strength, we will be weak in the Lord's strength.

God deliberately shares his power with the lowly, who have no power. With the proud, God stands far off, allowing them the results of a pride-filled existence.

When we cry out to God, he stretches forth his hand against our enemies.

Lord, you are the high and holy one. And yet you readily condescend to lift the lowly while deafening your ears to the proud and haughty. You come to me in the midst of my trouble, stretching forth your hand to revive me. By your right hand, I am saved. Father, it is worth being lowly because that's where I will find you.

Today's Takeaway

God takes note of the lowly, but he knows the proud afar off.

God Is the Perfecter of All That Concerns Me

The LORD will perfect that which concerneth me:
thy mercy, O LORD, endureth for ever: forsake
not the works of thine own hands.

PSALM 138:8

God has an active role in the life of every believer. And his work for each of us is a *perfect* work. The Lord sees where he wants to take us and arranges life's circumstances to bring us fully there.

The life of faith is a life that recognizes that we are the work of his hands and that his will for us is a perfect will. This gives us confidence to take the next step with courage.

God, I see through a glass darkly. What seems random, muddled—even confusing—is yet designed to perfect me. There are no unplanned incidents in my life. What happens to me, when acknowledged with faith, turns to my good. My plans seem short-range, and I desire quick resolutions to my troubles. But your plans for me are often long-range and require patience on my part. Lord, I bow to your perfect plan for me. You know best.

Today's Takeaway

God is always at work perfecting that which concerns me.

Fearfully and Wonderfully Made

I will praise thee; for I am fearfully and wonderfully made: marvelous are thy works; and that my soul knoweth right well. My substance was not hid from thee, when I was made in secret, and curiously wrought in the lowest parts of the earth. Thine eyes did see my substance, yet being unperfect; and in thy book all my members were written, which in continuance were fashioned, when as yet there was none of them.

Psalm 139:14-16

Have you thanked God lately for his care in creating you in your mother's womb? You were made by the Lord, in his image and carefully woven together to form a unique you.

From the top of your head to the bottom of your feet, you were designed by the Creator of the universe. The psalmist knew "right well," as do we, that our very creation necessitates praise.

Thank you, Father, for creating me, overseeing every aspect of my conception. Yes, I am fearfully and wonderfully handcrafted by you. In your book all my members were written; I was fashioned by you when I was made in the secrecy of my mother's womb. O Lord, marvelous are thy works indeed!

Today's Takeaway

God took great care in forming me in my mother's womb. He made no mistakes.

The Lord Covers My Head in Battle

O God the Lord, the strength of my salvation, thou hast covered my head in the day of battle. Grant not, O Lord, the desires of the wicked: further not his wicked device; lest they exalt themselves.

Psalm 140:7-8

The enemy of our soul never sleeps. He has waged constant war on us and keeps designing new strategies to bring us down. But God covers our heads in battle. He keeps us from falling as we trust in him.

Thus we pray with the psalmist that devices of the wicked one will not prevail against us.

The Lord answers that prayer with a decided yes—and a reminder that our enemy was defeated at the cross.

We now must walk out that victory.

Father, I praise you today for the helmet you've put on my head in the day of battle. In you, I am the victor in every skirmish. My enemy's desire falls to the ground as it meets your guardianship over me. There shall be no exaltation of the enemy with you as my protector.

Thank you, Lord!

Today's Takeaway

God covers my head in the battle.

Incense and Sacrifice

Lord, I cry unto thee: make haste unto me; give
ear unto my voice, when I cry unto thee.
Let my prayer be set forth before thee as incense;
and the lifting up of my hands as the evening sacrifice.
Psalm 141:1-2

God is never resentful of our prayers. They are to him as sweet-smelling incense. In the lifting of our hands in praise, God sees sacrifice. It's as if our hands lifted in surrender are his to do with as he will, so he may use our hands to perform the works he has prepared for us to do.

The psalmist often cried to the Lord. We might think God grows weary of hearing the psalmist—or us—cry out to him time after time... but that's not true. We were created for fellowship with God, and nothing summons the Lord's presence like a situation that compels us to cry out to him. So don't be shy about crying out to God time after time. He welcomes it.

Lord, may my every prayer be as incense to you. May my requests be in keeping with your Word. As I lift my hands to you, accept my surrender to your will. Accept, too, these hands to minister to those you send my way. Guard my hands from uses that are not in keeping with your will. Accept, O God, my sacrifice.

Today's Takeaway

My prayers are like sweet-smelling incense to the Lord.

Lord, My Tongue

Set a watch, O Lord, before my mouth; keep the door of my lips.

Psalm 141:3

Both the Old and the New Testament contain many admonitions about guarding our tongues. How easily we find fault with others and speak out when we should instead remain silent and pray.

How ready we are to give unwanted advice to others. Sometimes even our words to God need guarding, lest we say, "Why, Lord?" or "But God..."

The truth is our tongues need taming. Our mouths need to speak words that heal wounds, praise others, and comfort the afflicted. Just as we were converted, so do our tongues need to be converted.

Father, I have surrendered my hands and my heart to you. Accept also my mouth, lest I speak empty or hurting words. Put a watch over my lips so that I speak words that heal, encourage, and build up others. Tame my tongue, O Lord!

Today's Takeaway

My tongue is submitted to God for his purposes.

LORD, SET ME APART FROM EVIL

Incline not my heart to any evil thing,
to practice wicked works with men that work
iniquity: and let me not eat of their dainties.
PSALM 141:4

Evil often comes to us in a pretty package. Satan's poison is sweet to the taste. Our hearts are thus easily inclined to the evil one's "dainties" without thinking twice.

We can experience the sad result of following evil. Or, like the psalmist, we can pray that God would not incline our hearts to any evil thing, nor allow us to practice any wicked works.

How much wiser to avoid evil altogether than to learn the hard way by partaking of the enemy's poisonous dainties.

God, truth be known, I'm not always aware of the evil behind certain attractions to my flesh. What may look good to me may be candy laced with poison. So, O Lord, incline my heart not to evil but only to good. Give me discernment so I can more quickly recognize evil attractions before I partake of the "dainties."

Today's Takeaway

My heart is inclined to God, not to evil attractions.

I Poured Out My Complaint

I cried unto the Lord with my voice; with my voice
unto the Lord did I make my supplication.
I poured out my complaint before him; I showed before him my trouble.
When my spirit was overwhelmed within me, then thou knewest my path. In the way wherein I walked have they privily laid a snare for me.
Psalm 142:1-3

God accepts even our complaints in prayer. He hears our cries when we are overwhelmed. He sees the snares set on our path ahead.

Because God is sovereign, we can call on him and know he can bring remedy to our situation. Never be shy about pouring your heart out before the Lord.

He welcomes our cries.

O God, how easily my spirit is overwhelmed. But you saw my frustration and came to my rescue. Lord, you never fail when I honestly pour out my complaint to you. You even see the enemy's snare on the path ahead and warn me. So, my God, continually do I pray for your guidance and protection against the many snares of the enemy. Be there for me always, Lord.

Today's Takeaway

God hears my complaints and listens when I am overwhelmed.

Meditating and Musing

I remember the days of old; I meditate on all thy works; I muse on the work of thy hands. I stretch forth my hands unto thee: my soul thirsteth after thee, as a thirsty land. Selah. Hear me speedily, O Lord: my spirit faileth: hide not thy face from me, lest I be like unto them that go down into the pit. Cause me to hear thy lovingkindness in the morning; for in thee do I trust: cause me to know the way wherein I should walk; for I lift up my soul unto thee.

Psalm 143:5-8

Remembering our days of old and musing on the work of God's hands is healing to us. It's in recalling our history with the Lord that we're able to know he will guard our future as he has guarded us in the past.

Likewise, meditating on all his works brings a fresh amazement at the power, wisdom, and love of God.

We note that the desperate psalmist asks God to "cause" him to hear his loving-kindness in the morning and "cause" him to know the way wherein he should walk. That's a petition we all most earnestly pray since, if left to ourselves, we might easily wander off our designated path.

Lord, I love to recall past victories, of which there are many. I meditate on your goodness, and I consider the work of your hands. Your deeds call to mind your graciousness and love. Help me remember that today will one day be one of my "days of old" in which I will recall your present faithfulness.

Today's Takeaway

I enjoy meditating on the Lord's goodness to me.

Guide Me to the Land of Uprightness

Deliver me, O Lord, from mine enemies: I flee unto thee to hide me. Teach me to do thy will; for thou art my God: thy spirit is good; lead me into the land of uprightness. Quicken me, O Lord, for thy name's sake: for thy righteousness' sake bring my soul out of trouble.

Psalm 143:9-11

God is our leader in all things. He teaches us to do his will, and he guides us into uprightness. But to experience his leading we must forsake our own sense of direction. The Lord knows far better than we which path to take.

Our God is also our deliverer from our enemies. We flee to him for protection. We boldly ask him to bring our souls out of trouble—and he will.

God, you are many things to me, but in the day of trouble, you are my deliverer from my enemies. You bring my soul out of trouble. When I flee to you, I find safety from the storm.

Teach me, O Lord, to do your will, for you are my God. Lead me safely into the land of uprightness, though I dwell in a land of unrighteousness.

Today's Takeaway

As God leads me into the land of uprightness, I follow.

My Warring Hands

Blessed be the LORD my strength which teacheth my hands to war, and my fingers to fight.

PSALM 144:1

Sometimes life is a battle zone. War has been waged, and it's up to us to fight. But our carnal weapons are easily defeated by an overpowering enemy. What then?

Just this: God must teach us how to wage war and win. Our weapon is the sword of the Spirit. We can push back and even defeat the enemy by learning from the Lord how to fight, not in the natural but in the supernatural, where our true battle exists. God's warriors are not without weaponry!

We are victors. We need only to remember the source of our strength and employ our mighty spiritual weapons.

Lord, you see me when all is well, and you see me when my life is a war zone. On days when the latter is the case, you teach me how to fight back against the enemy's attacks. You strengthen my hands and teach them how to war. My fingers, under your command, are vigorous weapons.

Today's Takeaway

In my every war, I am a victor.

My Days Are as a Shadow

Lord, what is man, that thou takest knowledge of him!
or the son of man, that thou makest account of him!
Man is like to vanity: his days are as a shadow that passeth away.
Psalm 144:3-4

Our days here are few, our bodies weak. We are, after all, but humans. And yet the God of the universe has taken note of us. We who are little are loved by the One who is all powerful.

The contemplation of humankind in the light of God's omnipotence staggers the mind, but it gives us a secure hope. The Lord has noticed every sparrow that has fallen. He numbers the hairs on our heads. How, then, can we not be amazed that he takes note of each of us, calling us by name?

Lord, I marvel at all of your creation but especially your human creations. Though we are as dust, you prize us. So valuable are we that you gave your Son to prove our worth. How, then, can we ever be vain or claim to be a "self-made" success? You hold all the keys to life—both the natural life and the spiritual life. You are thus worthy of honor and praise!

Today's Takeaway

Though I am as a shadow that passes away, God takes note of me.

Happy Am I

Happy is that people, that is in such a case:
yea, happy is that people, whose God is the Lord.

Psalm 144:15

Happiness is God's open secret. All who would be happy must have God as their Lord. Belief in God, however, is not enough. Trust in the Lord—no matter what—brings us through great trials and finds us happy in God's care. If you have any doubts, ask Job. His latter end was far better after he suffered the greatest of trials. Or ask any of the disciples who suffered intensely for their faith but did so happily. History is a long line of Christians who went through the fires of life, enduring physical pain but counting themselves blessed to suffer for Christ. Faith triumphs over whatever life brings and assures happiness for those whose God is the Lord.

Lord, like everyone, I want to be happy, and true happiness starts with a relationship with you. Full surrender is the pathway to fulfillment. I think of Job and his awful tragedy...and yet his latter end was far better than his earlier years. The secret must be that even tragedies have their end. Nothing lasts forever. There is joy in waiting patiently, trusting in you. Yes, happy is that people who call you Lord. Happy, then, am I.

Today's Takeaway

God is my Lord. I am his—thus I am happy.

The Slowness of God's Anger

The Lord is gracious, and full of compassion;
slow to anger, and of great mercy.
The Lord is good to all: and his tender mercies are over all his works.
Psalm 145:8-9

We are prone to easy anger. God is not. The Lord is slow to anger, his mercy trumping his ire.

We often lack compassion for others in dire straits. God is full of compassion.

We are not always merciful. God's tender mercies are over all his works.

Yes, he is good to all. Even to his enemies—among whom we must count ourselves before our salvation. He has left us an example of loving *our* enemies. Such a person has surely known the Lord.

O gracious and compassionate God, how I praise you for your slowness to anger. Your great and tender mercies are over all your works, including me. Fill me with your compassion. Reproduce your tender mercies in me. Slow me down when I'm tempted to anger. Help me love my enemies. Fill me, Lord, with yourself.

Today's Takeaway

My God is compassionate, slow to anger, and of great mercy.

God, My Lifter

The Lord upholdeth all that fall, and raiseth up all those that be bowed down.
Psalm 145:14

When we take a fall, when we are unexpectedly bowed down, we need a hand up. God sees us when we stumble and offers the strong hand we need to rise again.

If we would emulate God, we, too, should look for those who have fallen and those who are bowed down, offering them our strong hands. If we are the fallen ones, we need only to ask and to reach up. God's hand is already extended. In his powerful grip, we rise again and again.

Lord, you uphold me. You bring me up when I am down. I pray to be like you in lifting up those who are down. It seems there are so many who are anxious, worried, stressed, or depressed. I want to offer them what you've given to me. Father, multiply your graces in me so I have grace to offer to others.

Today's Takeaway

God is there to pick me up when I stumble.

God's Open Hand

Thou openest thine hand, and satisfiest the desire of every living thing.
The Lord is righteous in all his ways, and holy in all his works.
The Lord is nigh unto all them that call upon
him, to all that call upon him in truth.
He will fulfil the desire of them that fear him: he
also will hear their cry, and will save them.
Psalm 145:16-19

God's hand is never closed to his children. He hears their cry and opens his hand to satisfy our desires. He is ever blessing his people. Why, then, would we ever turn to the pleasures of this world, pleasures that can never satisfy? The Lord desires to fill us with good things. Will we look up and see his open hand of blessing?

Lord, I see your open hand and the blessings you pour out for me. You satisfy my desires as you draw nigh to me. Indeed, your presence is my utmost desire. You hear my cry, Father, and you hasten to help me. O God, you are righteous in all your ways and holy in all your works. Blessed be your name!

Today's Takeaway

God's open hand brings me untold blessings.

My Happy Hope

Happy is he that hath the God of Jacob for his help, whose hope is in the Lord his God.
Psalm 146:5

Unhappiness happens. But such should only be shallow and only last for a season. On a deeper level there exists in the heart of every believer a reservoir of happiness made possible by the presence of God. Hard times come, but hard times go. Jacob didn't have an easy life by any means. And yet we're told by the psalmist that happy is the person who has the God of Jacob for his help. If your life has rough patches as did Jacob's, hang on. His God and yours will bring eventual happiness.

God of Jacob and of me, I bless your name! You are worthy of all praise. You bring happiness where there is sadness. You replace strife with peace. You trade the dark clouds of depression for unspeakable joy. Into the dry desert you bring springs of living water. Best of all, you bring all of these and more "free for the asking." O Lord, you know I do ask!

Today's Takeaway

My hope in the Lord renders me happy.

My Unlimited God Is Great

Praise ye the Lord: for it is good to sing praises unto
our God; for it is pleasant; and praise is comely.
The Lord doth build up Jerusalem: he gathereth
together the outcasts of Israel.
He healeth the broken in heart, and bindeth up their wounds.
He telleth the number of the stars; he calleth them all by their names.
Great is our Lord, and of great power: his understanding is infinite.
Psalm 147:1-5

Putting limits on God is an impossible task. His power, presence, and purpose are beyond our comprehension. Jesus reminds us that with God nothing is impossible. Do we believe that? If so, let's move ahead in life, confident in our omnipotent God.

O Lord, I love the fact that you know your universe so well that you recognize each star and call it by name. Praising you is so appropriate, for you not only know your creation but you care for it as well. You gather the outcasts, heal the brokenhearted, and bind up their wounds. You are the God who sees all, knows all, and governs the universe with justice and mercy.

Today's Takeaway

Praising God is pleasant to me and fitting for the Lord.

Praise Ye the Lord

Praise ye the Lord. Praise ye the Lord from the heavens: praise him in the heights.
Praise ye him, all his angels: praise ye him, all his hosts.
Praise ye him, sun and moon: praise him, all ye stars of light.
Praise him, ye heavens of heavens, and ye waters that be above the heavens.
Let them praise the name of the Lord: for he commanded, and they were created.

Psalm 148:1-5

Praising God is healthy for our bodies, souls, and spirits. We join with all of creation in our worship of the Lord. Throughout this dark and mysterious universe, every atom of creation urges us to join in the praise of our Creator.

Don't fear getting lost in praise. *Do* get lost in praise. There you will find the power and presence of God.

O Lord, may we all praise you—yes, we who wear mortal flesh, but may all your glorious creation rise up in worship and praise. May your angels sing your praises. May the sun, moon, and stars give you glory. May the heavens and the waters bow before you, O mighty One who spoke all creation into existence. Glory to your name!

Today's Takeaway

All of the universe joins me in giving praise to God!

The High Praises

Praise ye the Lord. Sing unto the Lord a new song,
and his praise in the congregation of saints.
Let Israel rejoice in him that made him: let the
children of Zion be joyful in their King.
Let them praise his name in the dance: let them sing
praises unto him with the timbrel and harp.
For the Lord taketh pleasure in his people: he
will beautify the meek with salvation.
Let the saints be joyful in glory: let them sing aloud upon their beds.
Let the high praises of God be in their mouth,
and a two-edged sword in their hand.

Psalm 149:1-6

The joy of the Christian is knowing that God takes pleasure in each believer. We are never a bother to the Lord. He delights in us. In turn, we delight in him. We rejoice, we dance, we make music with the timbrel and harp, we are joyful in glory. Oh, let the high praises of God be in our mouth and the two-edged sword of the Lord be in our hand!

O God, I sing your high praises today! I sing unto you a new song. I rejoice in you, the God who has made me and who sustains me day by day. I even praise you in the dance, Lord! I praise you for taking pleasure in your people, offering salvation to all who will believe. Let us all therefore be joyful in glory. May we sing aloud from our bed. Praise you, Lord!

Today's Takeaway

The high praises of God are in my mouth.

LET EVERYTHING PRAISE!

Praise ye the LORD. Praise God in his sanctuary:
praise him in the firmament of his power.
Praise him for his mighty acts: praise him
according to his excellent greatness.
Praise him with the sound of the trumpet: praise
him with the psaltery and harp.
Praise him with the timbrel and dance: praise him
with stringed instruments and organs.
Praise him upon the loud cymbals: praise him
upon the high sounding cymbals.
Let every thing that hath breath praise the LORD. Praise ye the LORD.

PSALM 150:1-6

Do you have breath? Then praise ye the Lord! And for what are we praising him? For his mighty acts! And each one of us is a mighty act of God. In what ways can you praise him? With music? With good deeds? With compassion and kindness? Whatever the Lord gives you in talents, skills, or interests can be instruments of praise. May we always praise our great God.

Lord, I love that the book of Psalms ends on the high note of praising you. There is no end to the many reasons to glorify you. The psalmists covered many, but there are always fresh reasons to praise you. Today, I thank you for this day...and all my future days until you receive me into heaven. Until then, I will always be one who praises God. Amen!

Today's Takeaway

I will worship my God while I still have breath.

About the Author

Nick Harrison is the author of more than a dozen books, including *The One Year Life Recovery Prayer Devotional, Magnificent Prayer, Power in the Promises, KJV Devotional for Men, KJV Devotional in the Morning and in the Evening,* and five books in the One-Minute® Prayer series. Nick and his wife, Beverly, are the parents of three grown daughters and grandparents to two boys and two girls.

More Great Devotionals from Nick Harrison

ONE-MINUTE PRAYERS® WHEN YOU NEED A MIRACLE

When life looks bleak and you need God to show up in a big way, *One-Minute Prayers® When You Need a Miracle* connects your needs to God's promises as time in prayer stretches your faith and enlarges your view of God.

ONE-MINUTE PRAYERS® FOR HUSBANDS

Discover biblical encouragement in this collection of prayers and devotions written for busy husbands who need a minute of inspiration.

ONE-MINUTE PRAYERS® FOR DADS

These brief prayers will help dads connect with God as they thank Him for their kids and ask Him for what they need to be the best fathers they can be.

ONE-MINUTE PRAYERS® FOR THOSE WITH CANCER

These encouraging writings will lead readers from fear to faith in the face of illness.

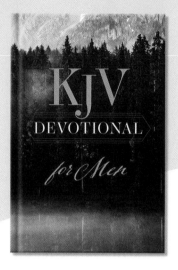

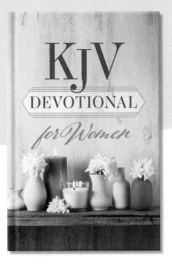

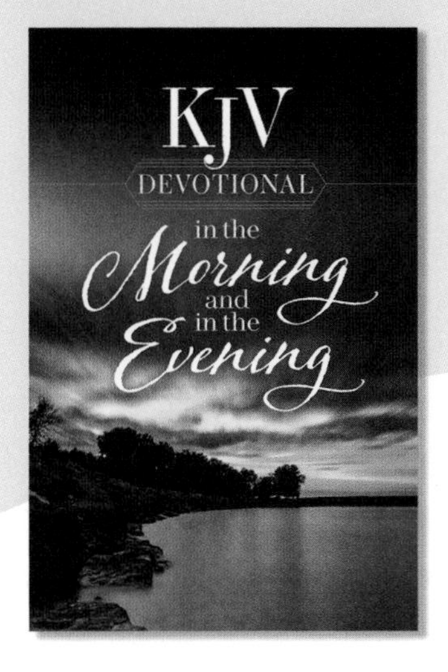

Twice-Daily Inspiration

A wonderful way to bookend each day, ***KJV Devotional in the Morning and in the Evening*** features eloquently written Scripture verses, quotes, and short spiritual applications that offer insights on…

Sustaining Faith—*O, love the* L*ORD, all ye his saints; for the* L*ORD preserveth the faithful* (Psalm 31:23).

Unspeakable Love—*Thanks be unto God for his unspeakable gift* (2 Corinthians 9:15).

Abundant Grace—*He giveth more grace. Wherefore he saith, God resisteth the proud, but giveth grace unto the humble* (James 4:6).

Perfect for gift-giving or personal study.

Available wherever books are sold.

To learn more about Harvest House books and to read sample chapters, visit our website:

www.HarvestHousePublishers.com